D0471370

THE
EIFFEL
TOWER

BUILDING
HISTORY
SERIES

THE EIFFEL TOWER

by Meg Greene

Lucent Books. Inc.. San Diego, California

Library of Congress Cataloging-in-Publication Data

Greene, Meg.
  The Eiffel Tower / by Meg Greene.
    p. cm. — (Building history series)
  Includes bibliographical references (p.   ) and index.
  ISBN 1-56006-826-4 (lib. : alk. paper)
  1. Touring Eiffel (Paris, France)—Juvenile literature. 2. Civil
engineering—France—Paris—History—Juvenile literature. 3. Civil
engineers—France—Biography—Juvenile literature. 4. Eiffel,
Gustave, 1832–1923—Juvenile literature. [1. Tour Eiffel (Paris,
France) 2. Eiffel Gustave, 1832–1923. 3. France—History—19th
century.] I. Title. II. Series.
  TA149 .G74 2001
  725'.97'0944361—dc21

                                                          00-010407

Copyright 2001 by Lucent Books, Inc.
P.O. Box 289011, San Diego, California, 92198-9011

Printed in the U.S.A.

CONTENTS

FOREWORD

Throughout history, as civilizations have evolved and prospered, each has produced unique buildings and architectural styles. Combining the need for both utility and artistic expression, a society's buildings, particularly its large-scale public structures, often reflect the individual character traits that distinguish it from other societies. In a very real sense, then, buildings express a society's values and unique characteristics in tangible form. As scholar Anita Abramovitz comments in her book *People and Spaces*, "Our ways of living and thinking—our habits, needs, fear of enemies, aspirations, materialistic concerns, and religious beliefs—have influenced the kinds of spaces that we build and that later surround and include us."

That specific types and styles of structures constitute an outward expression of the spirit of an individual people or era can be seen in the diverse ways that various societies have built palaces, fortresses, tombs, churches, government buildings, sports arenas, public works, and other such monuments. The ancient Greeks, for instance, were a supremely rational people who originated Western philosophy and science, including the atomic theory and the realization that the earth is a sphere. Their public buildings, epitomized by Athens's magnificent Parthenon temple, were equally rational, emphasizing order, harmony, reason, and above all, restraint.

By contrast, the Romans, who conquered and absorbed the Greek lands, were a highly practical people preoccupied with acquiring and wielding power over others. The Romans greatly admired and readily copied elements of Greek architecture, but modified and adapted them to their own needs. "Roman genius was called into action by the enormous practical needs of a world empire," wrote historian Edith Hamilton. "Rome met them magnificently. Buildings tremendous, indomitable, amphitheaters where eighty thousand could watch a spectacle, baths where three thousand could bathe at the same time."

In medieval Europe, God heavily influenced and motivated the people, and religion permeated all aspects of society, molding people's worldviews and guiding their everyday actions. That spiritual mindset is reflected in the most important medieval structure—the Gothic cathedral—which, in a sense, was a model of heavenly cities. As scholar Anne Fremantle so elegantly phrases it, the cathedrals were "harmonious elevations of stone and glass reaching up to heaven to seek and receive the light [of God]."

Our more secular modern age, in contrast, is driven by the realities of a global economy, advanced technology, and mass communications. Responding to the needs of international trade and the growth of cities housing millions of people, today's builders construct engineering marvels, among them towering skyscrapers of steel and glass, mammoth marine canals, and huge and elaborate rapid transit systems, all of which would have left their ancestors, even the Romans, awestruck.

In examining some of humanity's greatest edifices, Lucent Books' Building History series recognizes this close relationship between a society's historical character and its buildings. Each volume in the series begins with a historical sketch of the people who erected the edifice, exploring their major achievements as well as the beliefs, customs, and societal needs that dictated the variety, functions, and styles of their buildings. A detailed explanation of how the selected structure was conceived, designed, and built, to the extent that this information is known, makes up the majority of the volume.

Each volume in the Lucent Building History series also includes several special features that are useful tools for additional research. A chronology of important dates gives students an overview, at a glance, of the evolution and use of the structure described. Sidebars create a broader context by adding further details on some of the architects, engineers, and construction tools, materials, and methods that made each structure a reality, as well as the social, political, and/or religious leaders and movements that inspired its creation. Useful maps help the reader locate the nations, cities, streets, and individual structures mentioned in the text; and numerous diagrams and pictures illustrate tools and devices that bring to life various stages of construction. Finally, each volume contains two bibliographies, one for student research, the other listing works the author consulted in compiling the book.

Taken as a whole, these volumes, covering diverse ancient and modern structures, constitute not only a valuable research tool, but also a tribute to the human spirit, a fascinating exploration of the dreams, skills, ingenuity, and dogged determination of the great peoples who shaped history.

Important Dates in the Building of the Eiffel Tower

1889
The tower is completed almost two months ahead of schedule.

1915–1918
The Eiffel Tower is closed during World War I.

1900
The Eiffel Tower becomes part of the 1900 Paris Universal Exposition.

1886
Gustave Eiffel wins the design competition for the 1889 Centennial Exposition, sponsored by the French government.

1903
Gustave Eiffel begins a series of research experiments on aerodynamics at the tower.

| 1880 | 1890 | 1900 | 1910 | 1920 |

1889
The Centennial Exposition opens on May 7, 1889.

1887
Construction begins on the Eiffel Tower.

1898
The Eiffel Tower is used for early radio transmitting exercises.

The Centennial Exposition opened on May 7, 1889, with the Eiffel Tower as its centerpiece.

1945
The tower houses France's first civil radio station.

1921
First European public radio broadcast is done from the tower.

1947
The tower has a million visitors for the first time since 1900.

Vendors at the base of the Eiffel Tower sell ice cream to tourists.

1923
Gustave Eiffel dies at the age of ninety-one.

1996
The tower briefly closes due to a workers' strike.

| 1920 | 1940 | 1950 | 1990 | 2000 |

1925
Early television experiments are held at the Eiffel Tower.

1999
The tower hosts a spectacular millennium celebration.

1940–1944
The tower is closed except to German soldiers.

1989
The tower's hundredth anniversary is celebrated; over five million people visit.

1953
The country's first television station begins operations from the Eiffel Tower.

INTRODUCTION

The idea of building tall towers and buildings is not new. Since ancient times, human beings have dreamed of designing and building structures that towered above the earth and soared toward the heavens. For many people, there is something exhilarating about structures, natural or human-made, that rise great heights, dominating the landscape below.

With the development of new building materials such as iron and later steel and reinforced concrete, and the advancement of engineering technology beginning in the early nineteenth century, architects contemplated designing and building taller structures. The competition among nations to construct the tallest structures soon became an important symbol of technological superiority. Whichever country had the most advanced technology was sure to surpass its rivals, not just in building, but also in manufacturing, commerce, and warfare.

THE FIRST TOWERS

Almost all cultures have built towers of one sort or another. Among the first towers were the *ziggurats*, or "heavenly mountains," built in ancient Mesopotamia as early as 2200 B.C.. Constructed of spe-

The ziggurats of ancient Mesopotamia were among the world's first towers.

cial bricks, some of which were eight feet thick, these legendary structures measured up to 335 square feet at the base and rose as high as 170 feet. The ziggurats were religious temples in which the pious made offerings to the gods. For many cultures, towers also became the means to honor a god or to serve as a place of worship. Towers, then, were important as expressions of spiritual life as well as technical and architectural achievement.

The pyramids of Egypt, built as early as 2650 B.C., testify to the architectural skills of the Egyptians. Unlike the ziggurats, which were built to honor the gods, the pyramids were tombs constructed to commemorate the pharaohs who had commissioned them. The largest of these structures, the "Great Pyramid," is 481 feet high, with a base that covers almost 13 acres.

Ancient builders, though, were limited in the kinds of materials and techniques available to them. For centuries they had only clay bricks, stone, and wood at their disposal. The limitations of these materials and technologies obviously curtailed the height of their structures. But as building methods, materials, and technology became more sophisticated, so, too, did the buildings themselves.

The attempt to build taller and more majestic buildings succeeded brilliantly during the Middle Ages. Medieval builders developed a new building system based on the use of skeletal framing, which allowed for the construction of the majestic spires and towers that characterize many Gothic cathedrals. A common type of tower, which came to be known as the *campanile*, or large bell tower, was attached to many churches and monasteries beginning in the sixth century.

Christians were not alone in mastering the architecture of the tower, however. Muslims built minarets, a high slender tower often attached to a mosque upon which a man called a muezzin stood to summon the faithful to prayer. Buddhists, too, built tall pagodas, some measuring as high as 492 feet.

Yet the construction of tall buildings and towers was not only a reflection of spiritual longing and the quest for salvation in the next world, it was also a statement of power, status, and wealth in the here and now. Almost immediately rulers and their military advisors realized the value of towers as lookout posts. Many towers constructed within castles were also meant to intimidate enemies with their sheer size and bulk. Elaborate towers that often dominated palaces or town commons were as much displays

Hsinbyume Pagoda in Mingun, Myanmar, is a magnificent Buddhist religious monument.

of material prosperity and wealth as they were of spiritual, artistic, or military value.

Other towers, though, served purely practical functions. For example, the many lighthouses that dotted the world's coastlines had to be tall so incoming sailors could see their warning beacons. And windmills needed to be of a certain height if they were to operate properly.

As architecture progressed, however, builders became more intent not only on making towers taller but on designing unique structures that showcased the new technology. By the nineteenth century, the building of towers and magnificent one-of-a-kind buildings symbolized the new age of technological and industrial progress.

THE INDUSTRIAL FAIR

As industrial technology spread, many European countries found themselves competing with each other to develop the best machines and processes to put these machines to the most innovative and efficient use. Eventually, the idea of holding industrial fairs at which various countries could showcase their discoveries and advancements became an important aspect of nineteenth-century European, and later American, culture.

Great Britain, the first country to industrialize, was also the first to host an industrial world's fair. In 1849, Prince Albert, the husband of Queen Victoria and president of the Royal Society of Arts, invited representatives from a number of industrialized countries to participate in an exposition. Hoping to have their exhibits displayed at what promised to be a spectacular international event, more than thirteen thousand individuals responded. The exhibition opened at the Crystal Palace in Hyde Park, London, on May 1, 1851, to great fanfare and excitement.

No doubt the greatest attraction of the industrial fair was the Crystal Palace itself, which Sir Joseph Paxton had designed especially for the occasion. The building was a remarkable piece of construction for the time. Built from prefabricated parts, or pieces that had been made ahead of time and then assembled, the Crystal Palace was a rectangular structure 1,851 feet long, 456 feet wide, 66 feet high, and enclosing almost 1 million square feet of floor space. Projecting from the middle of

London's Crystal Palace, built in 1851, exhibited many new inventions in the Machinery Court.

the building was a dramatic, vaulted transept, or high-ceilinged arched hallway. This hallway consisted of an intricate network of slender iron rods supporting walls of clear glass. The main floor and galleries of the Crystal Palace had room for more than eight miles of display tables on which the chosen exhibitors unveiled their inventions. Among the exhibits were false teeth, artificial legs, firearms, rubber goods, chewing tobacco, and farming implements.

More than 6 million visitors attended the exhibition, making it a great financial success for the British. The Crystal Palace also established the architectural standard for buildings at later industrial fairs. Indeed, these later fairs would not so much promote business directly as display technological developments and encourage manufacturers to compete with each other by offering competitive awards and prizes. Hailed as one of Britain's finest monuments, the Crystal Palace represented the start of a new round of technological, industrial, and economic competition among the nations of Europe.

A WONDROUS AGE

As the technology of the period became more advanced, exhibition buildings and demonstrations also became more sophisticated and elaborate. For architects, the new ways of building and the use of new construction materials allowed for the design of more intricate and daring structures. For visitors, the industrial fairs presented a remarkable opportunity to glimpse the future. For both, almost anything seemed possible; only a lack of imagination could limit what the human mind could create and what human beings could accomplish.

It was the French exposition of 1889 that, with the spectacular Eiffel Tower, gave the world not only its first view of French technology but also an indication of the future of construction. For some, the tower was an iron monstrosity. For others, though, it captured the ideal of every builder who had ever dreamed of designing and building the perfect structure. The Eiffel Tower impressed the millions who attended the fair with its dizzying height and its unconventional use of materials. More than that though, the Eiffel Tower, according to one art historian, "engaged millions of people from the nation and the world in an experience that touched their imaginations and sensibilities."[1]

THE IDEA OF A TOWER

During the late nineteenth century, France's devastating defeat suffered at the hands of the Prussians in the Franco-Prussian War of 1870 to 1871 was still a bitter memory to many Frenchmen. This conflict brought about the national unification of Germany and resulted in the collapse of the government of Emperor Napoléon III. The Prussian victory also cost France Alsace and Lorraine, two industrialized provinces situated along the border with Germany. To make matters worse, the Treaty of Frankfurt, drafted in May 1871 and ending the war, demanded that the French government make reparation payments in the amount of almost five billion francs, or approximately one billion dollars. Until the debt was paid, German troops would continue to occupy eastern France.

To help make the reparation payments, the new French president, Adolphe Thiers, demanded the collection of rents and debts that had been suspended in France during the war. At the same time, Thiers decided to save additional funds by not paying national guardsmen. The institution of these two policies meant that many Parisian families, left nearly destitute by the war, had no money to pay for food, housing, and other essentials. Tensions mounted as creditors pressed for payment of the money owed to them.

THE COMMUNARDS

The situation was intolerable. Members of the Paris Commune, a group of socialists, anarchists, and nationalists who had opposed the peace settlement with Prussia, simply refused to obey President Thiers's decree. Instead, the Communards, as they were called, took to the streets of Paris in protest and, in the end, managed to seize control of a large portion of the city. For two months 30,000 Communards held out against 130,000 government troops. The Communards went on a rampage of slaughter and destruction. They set fire to numerous public buildings and came very close to demolishing the cathedral of

Communards, those who opposed the peace settlement with Prussia, execute their political hostages.

Notre-Dame and the Louvre. But when the Communards began to lynch prisoners and execute hostages, Thiers sent in troops to quell the uprising.

The spectacle that greeted the troops as they entered Paris infuriated them. Roofs of houses were missing, stores had been looted and burned, and the streets were littered with the bodies of the dead. In retaliation, the army launched a massacre of its own. The bloodbath was appalling. Between May 21 and May 28, 1871, government troops killed or executed without trial an estimated 20,000 Communards. Others were sentenced to long terms in French penal colonies such as Devil's Island, a notorious prison located on a French island off the coast of South America.

The brutal fighting between government troops and the Communards left whole sections of Paris in ruins, presenting, according to some eyewitnesses, a desolate landscape of "gaping roofs, battered walls, and charred frontage. . . . The theaters were closed and the shops were shuttered."[2] It seemed that the city and the nation would never return to normal.

THE BELLE EPOQUE

Under the leadership of President Thiers, however, France gradually regained its stability and recovered its prosperity. By the end of the decade, the country was poised to enter what would become known in French history as the "Belle Epoque," or the "beautiful years."

"War, revolutions, military intrigues, strategy, tactics, artillery, shells, petrol, we've had enough of them,"[3] wrote a popular French journalist of the time. Music, talk, and laughter filled the parks and cafes of the once decimated city. The theater and opera played to packed houses, while Parisians strolled contentedly down the Champs-Élysées or along the Seine River.

During the Belle Epoque the French economy grew strong and, as a result, the standard of living for many Frenchmen improved. A renewed affluence swept the country and people found they had more money to spend. The return of prosperity also meant more jobs and greater opportunities than ever before. The horrible deprivation that so many suffered just a few years earlier had all but disappeared.

Anxious to take advantage of the situation, the French government turned its attention overseas in the hope of establishing a colonial empire like that of Great Britain. During the 1880s, the French extended their influence to northern and central Africa, and to an area in Southeast Asia (then known as Indochina), which comprises modern-day Vietnam and Thailand. Within a decade, the French colonial empire grew to become the second largest in the world in terms of population and size. Only the British Empire surpassed it. The recovery was nothing short of remarkable for a nation that only a brief time before had stood vanquished by its enemies and divided against itself.

President Thiers governed France during the "Belle Epoque" period.

A WORLD POWER AGAIN

By the 1880s, then, the French were on the verge of reestab-
lishing their country as one of the world's leading powers.
Members of the French government searched for a way in
which to celebrate this happy turn of events, while making sure
that the leaders and people of rival countries recognized the
growing importance of France.

As early as 1878 government leaders had begun to discuss
commemorating the centennial of the French Revolution, which
would take place in 1889. Many thought that the festivities ought
to be kept to a minimum, with nothing too grand or flamboyant,
because as several cabinet members pointed out, the leaders of
other European countries still regarded France with suspicion,
considering it a hotbed of political radicalism and social instabil-
ity. Those nations might choose not to participate in an extravagant exposition venerating the French Revolution. Better perhaps
to stage a less elaborate ceremony than to risk the embarrassment
of being snubbed by the other world powers.

Other government officials, however, favored the idea of
holding a magnificent exposition. What better way to celebrate
the renewed prosperity and influence of France, they argued,
than with a spectacular industrial exhibition celebrating the
one-hundredth anniversary of the French Revolution. Prime
Minister Jules Ferry was among the most enthusiastic support-
ers of this proposal. He argued that not only would the event
commemorate the French Revolution, but it would also showcase present French power, wealth, and progress and would re-
veal to the world the great strides the French had made in
engineering and technology.

President Jules Grévy agreed, and on November 8, 1884,
signed a decree declaring that a "Universal Exposition of the
Products of Industry shall be opened in Paris May 5, 1889, and
closed October 31 following."[4] Little did anyone realize that the
proposed event would become one of the most successful and
memorable expositions ever held.

PLANNING THE EXHIBITION

The idea seemed simple enough. According to the initial report
by the French government, "The Exposition of 1889 will have
the character of a centennial exhibit, summing up what freedom
of work has produced in terms of progress during the last one

OTHER FRENCH EXPOSITIONS

Beginning in 1855 and continuing until 1900, the French staged a series of impressive world's fairs. Scheduled approximately every eleven years and always held in Paris, each of the expositions gained a reputation of being more spectacular than its predecessor. After the success of England's Crystal Palace Exhibition of 1851, Emperor Napoléon III vowed that future French expositions would be even greater and more brilliant.

The expositions were noted as much for their extravagant structures as they were for their amazing exhibits, which often showcased the latest technological innovations. The Paris Universal Exposition of 1855, for example, featured the great Palais de l'Industrie, constructed on the city of Paris's most famous avenue, the Champs-Élysées. The "cathedral of commerce," as it became known, was a rectangular structure with a glass nave, or central space. Measuring about 150 feet wide, more than twice that of England's Crystal Palace, the nave was surrounded on four sides by a double row of low aisles. The nave's glass vault rested on a series of arched, wrought-iron lattice girders. These girders consisted of two parallel metal beams linked by smaller metal bars arranged in a zigzag pattern. The girders were braced by lead supports called abutments. This impressive structure served as the model for exhibition buildings at later fairs such as the London Exposition of 1862 and the Chicago Exposition in 1893.

The main building of the 1867 exhibition, erected by Krantz and Alexandre Eiffel (who were not related to Gustave), was an oval-shaped structure measuring 1,608 feet high and 1,266 feet wide. It was divided into seven galleries, or exhibition spaces, with each sharing a central oblong open court. The outermost gallery, which housed the Galerie des Machines or Gallery of Machines, was the largest building at the fair, standing an impressive 82 feet high and 115 feet wide. Numerous smaller pavilions and towers were scattered about the principal building.

These expositions played an important role in French history. Not only did they provide entertainment to thousands, the expositions also demonstrated the rapid progress of French industry, which had for many years lagged behind other countries, especially Great Britain. These expositions did much to showcase the emergence of a France that was no longer a predominantly agricultural country but a blossoming industrial giant.

hundred years." The report went on to say that "1789 was a historic date in economics as well as politics, and it is to examine the world's economic situation that all nations are invited."[5]

By emphasizing the idea of technological and economic progress rather than the French Revolution itself, the Exposition Committee hoped to make the event more appealing so that other countries would be willing to participate. Still, the exposition would prove a hard sell as all nations were somewhat distrustful of French motives. In the end, several countries, including Austria-Hungary, Belgium, Great Britain, the Netherlands, and Germany, refused to participate. Instead, private citizens with no official aid or input from the government organized exhibits from those countries.

Despite initial French enthusiasm for the Centennial Exposition, it would take another three years for the government to finalize its plans. At last, in the spring of 1886, the Exposition Committee, with a budget of $8.6 million, set out to find an appropriate symbol for this great event.

It was Édouard Lockroy, the minister of commerce and industry and the chairman of the Exposition Committee, who proposed the construction of a thousand-foot tower as a fitting emblem for the fair. It is possible that Lockroy was thinking along the same lines as Georges Berger, a former commissioner for the International Exhibitions who had been appointed as the general manager of the Centennial Exposition. In outlining what the exposition hoped to accomplish, Berger declared that, "We will show . . . progress in knowledge, love of work, and respect for liberty."[6] Lockroy, like Berger, wanted nothing less than the most successful exposition ever. And for Lockroy, there was no better way to symbolize those goals than with the construction of a spectacular tower.

Observers noted that the idea of a tall tower was not a new one. Organizers of other expositions had attempted to build similar structures. In March 1833, for example, a British railroad engineer named Richard Trevithick had proposed the construction of a 1,000-foot tower to commemorate the passage of Britain's First Reform Bill (which increased the number of people who were eligible to vote) the previous year. The proposed structure was to be made of cast iron, 100 feet in diameter at the base and 10 feet across at the top. The tower would also have had a large statue crowning the tip. But when Trevithick died a month later, his plans for the tower died with him.

When Lockroy suggested his idea for the French exposition tower, the tallest tower standing in the world was the Washington Monument, completed in 1884. The obelisk-shaped monument, which soared to the astonishing height of 555 feet, however, was a far cry from the 1,000-foot structure that Lockroy envisioned and that many engineers dreamed of building.

THE COMPETITION

On May 2, 1886, the *Journal Officiel*, a publication of the French government, invited all French architects and engineers to submit designs for buildings and other attractions for the exposition. In addition, the notice invited all to "study the possibility of erecting on the Champ de Mars, a popular park in central Paris, an iron tower with a base 125 meters square and 300 meters high."[7] Although other designs would be considered, it was clear that the committee, and especially Lockroy, wished for a tower, specifically a metal one.

With the deadline for submissions set for May 18, applicants did not have much time to ready their blueprints. Despite the tight schedule, though, more than one hundred proposals arrived for the review of the committee, each vying for one of the twelve cash prizes awarded to the best designs. For three days, the projects would be on public display, and then the committee would make the final decision.

ÉDOUARD LOCKROY

Édouard Lockroy, the French minister of commerce and industry, proved an excellent choice to head the Centennial Exposition Committee. A graduate of the Beaux-Arts, a prestigious French art academy, Lockroy was also the author of several comedies and operettas, as well as an aspiring journalist. Known for his biting wit, Lockroy counted among his friends many of the leading French authors of the time, including Émile Zola and Victor Hugo. It was Lockroy who first sensed the possibilities of a tower after hearing Gustave Eiffel's presentation in 1885. He was also a powerful advocate of the Centennial Exposition from the time it was first proposed.

LIGHTING UP THE NIGHT SKY

One of the more innovative designs submitted for the Centennial Exposition competition came from two engineers who proposed a thousand-foot granite tower that would be topped by a powerful electric light. Surrounding the light would be a number of parabolic, or curved, mirrors to act as reflectors. So efficient would be this power source, its designers claimed, that people living even in the most remote sections of Paris would receive enough light to be able to read a newspaper at night. Not everyone was convinced that the idea would work, however. Upon hearing a description of the proposed light tower, a newspaper reporter of the time, quoted in Henri Loyette's book, *Gustave Eiffel,* quipped: "Given the height of our houses, the narrowness of our streets, and that fact that they rarely lie in line with the rays coming from the foot of the column, only the roofs would be brightly lit; so that by a reversal which the designers certainly did not intend, it will be the cats who see clearly and the passersby who will not see at all."

The designs ranged from the pedestrian to the preposterous. Working quickly, committee members sorted through the drawings. One entrant proposed a tower in the shape of a giant water sprinkler, which, the designer argued, could be used to water Paris in the event of a drought. Another design was in the shape of a giant guillotine that would have recalled the French Revolution more vividly than many would have liked. A design that received serious consideration was for the construction of a tower straddling the Seine River and linking the Champ de Mars, where the exposition was to be held, to the famous Trocadéro gardens. Officials were concerned, though, about the problems of laying a foundation for a structure that weighed thousands of tons directly on the riverbed. In the end, they rejected the proposal, citing the competition guidelines that the structure had to be built on the Champ de Mars itself.

THE WINNING DESIGN

When describing what he hoped for in the winning design, Commerce Minister Lockroy declared that "it should have a

well-defined character and appear as an original masterpiece of
the metals industry."[8] The winning design of the competition
came as close as possible to giving Lockroy what he envisioned.

The winner of the competition and the recipient of the eight
hundred dollar prize was no stranger to the field of engineering
or construction. Fifty-three-year-old Gustave Eiffel was already
regarded as one of the most innovative and masterful architectural engineers in France, with a reputation for constructing ex-
ceptional metal structures such as bridges and viaducts. The
winning design that Eiffel submitted consisted of an iron tower
that weighed approximately seven thousand tons with proposed
construction costs of $1.6 million.

The tower design Eiffel put forth was not a complete sur-
prise to Lockroy and the other members of the committee because they had seen it before. Eiffel's design first came to light

*Gustave Eiffel, a highly regarded architectural engineer, proposed that the
tower be the centerpiece for the 1889 exposition.*

almost two years earlier when drawings and diagrams had appeared in a French civil engineering review and a daily Parisian newspaper. This was not unusual, for Eiffel often published his drawings and diagrams so that other engineers and architects could see what he was doing. In May 1885, Eiffel outlined his proposal in an address delivered before the French Society of Civil Engineers. Shortly thereafter, upon hearing of the plans for a Centennial Exposition, Eiffel visited Lockroy and showed him the design. Eiffel suggested that the tower might make a spectacular centerpiece for the exposition of 1889. Lockroy never forgot Eiffel or the tower design. In fact, some historians have suggested that the committee formulated the criteria for the competition with Eiffel's tower in mind, right down to the precise measurements—125 meters (410 feet) square for the base and 300 meters (984 feet) for the height.

As the committee evaluated the submissions of other entrants, Lockroy named a subcommittee to determine whether such a structure could realistically be built. After examining all

WHO REALLY DESIGNED THE EIFFEL TOWER?

The plan for the Eiffel Tower was actually first committed to paper in the latter part of 1884. Upon hearing news of the forthcoming Centennial Exposition, Maurice Koechlin, chief of research at Gustave Eiffel's engineering company, set to work with a company engineer and a company architect to draw up plans for a tower. On June 6, 1884, he presented his sketch to Eiffel. The existence of this blueprint would later lead to allegations that Eiffel had stolen the idea from his colleague.

In fact, Eiffel always gave full credit to Koechlin for his role in the tower's design, although it was Eiffel's name that always came first when talking about the design's inception. Koechlin never took more credit for his role, either, always stating that he had done the first design, nothing more. The tower design was always advertised as a joint effort, for Eiffel's research team turned out several versions of a thousand-foot tower. It was Eiffel himself, however, who chose the final design, and who, in the end, assumed complete responsibility for its construction.

the designs, it appeared to the subcommittee that Eiffel's tower came closest to fulfilling the aesthetic, technical, economic, and symbolic requirements of the exposition.

Gustave Eiffel's own argument for his design was another compelling reason for Lockroy to give serious consideration to this tower. Eiffel stressed that the use of stone for a tower would place impossible constraints both in terms of time and money. He also believed that building creatively with stone was no longer possible. As he pointed out to the committee, earlier civilizations had built with stone. So had the great artisans of the Middle Ages and the Renaissance. For Eiffel, there appeared to be little left to try with stone as a means of building monumental structures. He stressed that this bold, new era in building and construction technology called for a new material: metal. According to Eiffel, only metal could give the tower the necessary appearance of "seem[ing] to spring out of the ground and somehow be molded by the action of the wind itself." Further, the proposed tower would symbolize "not only the art of the modern Engineer, but also the century of Industry and Science in which we are living."[9]

With the announcement of the winning design, the committee turned its attention to other pressing matters. Their task was finished. For Gustave Eiffel, though, the work had just begun.

According to Eiffel, the best building material for the proposed tower was metal.

An Engineering Genius

Alexandre-Gustave Eiffel, the first child and only son of François-Alexandre and Catherine-Melanie Eiffel, was born on December 15, 1832, in Dijon, France. His father was a soldier who had run away from his family's prosperous tapestry-making business at the age of sixteen to serve in the army of French general Napoléon Bonaparte. Wounded twice while fighting in Italy, François returned to France where he received orders to join the army stationed at Dijon. It was there that he met and later married Gustave's mother, the daughter of a wealthy lumber merchant.

In his later years, Eiffel recalled his childhood in Dijon as one of the happiest times of his life. His mother had a keen intelligence and encouraged him in all he did. It was she who provided him with his early education and who later helped him start his own business. Eiffel, in turn, was close to his mother throughout her life.

Madame Eiffel also proved to be a resourceful businesswoman. Writing about her, Eiffel declared that she was always "looking for some commercial employment which would provide the opportunity to open up a wider and more lucrative field for her energy and remarkable business sense."[10] She found it through the ownership of a series of coal-loading and storage stations and the operation of a shipping and delivery business. In time, Eiffel's parents sold the thriving business at a healthy profit.

Young Eiffel also looked forward to Sunday visits from his uncle Jean-Baptiste Mollerat, a successful chemist who had invented a process for distilling vinegar from wood. He greatly admired Uncle Mollerat, often visiting his home near the vinegar factory. There he passed many hours listening to stories and asking questions about his uncle's business. Eiffel was also drawn to another local chemist, Michel Perret, who, like Madame

Eiffel, owned a number of successful mines near Lyons. Eiffel often accompanied Perret to these mines, where he learned about chemistry and mining as well as religion and philosophy.

A Reluctant Student

For all his curiosity of mind, Eiffel was not especially studious. His parents had sent him to the nearby Lycée Royal (Royal School), where he proved to be anything but a star pupil. He hated the classes in which students had to memorize their lessons and found the school atmosphere confining. He later wrote that school left him with nothing but "the most wretched memories . . . [of] dreary classes, in which you were unspeakably bored and felt you were completely wasting your time."[11] It would not be until his last two years at the school that Eiffel finally found subjects that interested him. Thanks to the efforts of two of his teachers, he developed great enthusiasm for history and literature. His grades improved so much that Eiffel graduated with a double baccalaureate in literature and science.

From the Lycée Royal, Eiffel's parents sent him to Paris to study at the exclusive Sainte Barbé college, a school noted for its rigorous academic and technical programs. At Sainte Barbé, Eiffel was to prepare for the difficult entrance examinations to the prestigious École Polytechnique, or Technical College. Once

Eiffel recalled his childhood in Dijon, France (pictured), as being some of the happiest times in his life.

While living in Paris, one of Gustave Eiffel's favorite pastimes was swimming in the city's Seine River.

more, however, Eiffel was unenthusiastic about his studies. In a letter to his mother dated October 12, 1860, Eiffel complained:

> Here I am sitting at an oak table . . . in a classroom which is cold and quiet and almost empty. I can see nothing except the many windows of the building and the black walls of the [nearby] College Louis-le-Grand, instead of the lovely view I used to have from my window [at home] and so I am sad in spite of myself. . . . I am bored. . . . I think about Dijon and all the folks I have left there."[12]

In between his studies, Eiffel made the most of his time in Paris, taking in the sights. He enjoyed swimming in the Seine River, watching plays, visiting the great French art museum, the Louvre, and strolling to the Conservatoire des Arts et Métiers (School of Arts and Letters). Although not particularly fond of school, Eiffel liked Paris, finding himself drawn to the bright lights and bustling activities of the city. His mother was not pleased however, writing that "Gustave dreams of nothing but Paris."[13] She worried that he would eventually settle there instead of returning to Dijon.

To his parents' dismay, Eiffel was not motivated by any grand desire to study at the Polytechnique. This was just as well, for in 1852 he failed to gain entrance to the school. Although his parents were disappointed, Eiffel did not brood over his failure and wasted no time looking for an alternate plan. Not long afterward, he enrolled in the École Centrale des Arts et Manufactures. Unlike the semi-military and authoritarian atmosphere of the Polytechnique, the École Centrale was noted for its reputation as a liberal private school that still managed to turn out solid graduates in the fields of science and engineering. In time, it became known as one of the premier engineering schools in Europe.

Upon enrolling at the École Centrale, Eiffel immediately declared chemistry his major, for his uncle Mollerat had promised him a job as a chemist at his vinegar works in Dijon when he graduated. For the next three years, Eiffel applied himself. Although not outstanding, his grades were adequate. His only real obstacle was drawing class, where he struggled to make passing grades and later wrote that "the teacher gives me bad marks out of habit."[14]

In 1855, just before Eiffel received his degree, he learned of a quarrel between his parents and his uncle that would change the course of his life forever. Since his parents and his uncle no longer spoke to each other, Eiffel could hardly take the job his uncle had once offered him. He had to find other means of employment.

A CAREER DECIDED BY CHANCE

Eiffel was deeply disappointed by this turn of events. Having been assured of a job while in school, he now found himself unemployed with no job prospects in sight. Eventually, he took a position in an engineering firm headed by Charles Nepveu, who

POLYTECHNIQUE

For many upper-middle-class families in France, the opportunity to send a son to study at the prestigious Polytechnique was a welcomed prospect. Founded in 1795, the Polytechnique was known for its rigorous programs in mathematics and science. By the middle of the nineteenth century, the reputation of the Polytechnique was so widespread that similar programs appeared in such cities as Prague, Vienna, Zurich, and St. Petersburg. The Polytechnique was operated by the French state in a semi-military fashion. Graduates often went into government service, and for generations exercised a tremendous influence on the administration and management of the French government.

was an official of the French Society of Civil Engineers. Nepveu's company specialized in the construction of steam engines and other railroad equipment. Although Eiffel's training in chemistry was not much help to him in his new job, Nepveu liked him and offered to teach him the business. Eager to have the security of a steady income, Eiffel readily agreed. Nepveu hired him as his personal assistant at a monthly salary of about thirty dollars a month.

Unfortunately, the arrangement did not last long. Nepveu was a better engineer than a businessman. Only a few months after he hired Eiffel, Nepveu's company went bankrupt. Once again, Eiffel was out of a job. Fortunately, the Belgian firm that bought the company hired both Nepveu and Eiffel. In writing to his mother, Eiffel described his new job as chief of research: "I am engaged at the railroad office from 9:00 A.M. to 5:30 P.M. and I have a great deal of work there. . . . I am very well regarded and I am only . . . [sent] interesting tasks. I am now planning a sheet-metal bridge and I study almost every evening with my boss."[15]

Eiffel's hard work and determination eventually paid off. In September of 1856, his first design—a seventy-two-foot bridge to be constructed of cast and sheet iron—was accepted by the company.

THE FAST TRACK

In 1858, at the age of twenty-five, Eiffel received his first big job. Two French railway companies, the Compagnie d'Orléans and the Compagnie du Midi, decided to join their lines with a bridge near the city of Bordeaux that would span the Garonne River. Eiffel was given the great responsibility of overseeing the entire operation, which had been budgeted at six hundred thousand dollars. The two companies expected the project to be finished by June 1860, which gave him only two years to complete it.

Two years might have seemed like plenty of time, but Eiffel knew better. The proposed sixteen-hundred-foot-long bridge was to be constructed of cast iron, harder and more brittle than wrought iron. It was to rest on six piers, or square posts often made of stone or wood, to support the weight of a structure. If construction of the bridge itself were not daunting enough, it had to span one of the most turbulent rivers in France.

Working sixteen hours a day, Eiffel devised a plan to save time by introducing a new system of pile driving that he had begun to study when still working for Nepveu. Pile driving was the process of pushing a structure's foundation materials, such as wood logs, and later, steel posts, into soft ground. Eiffel proposed a system of hydraulic presses, machines that were operated by water, steam, and compressed air, to drive the piles into the eighty-foot-deep river.

Eiffel's method proved as effective as he had hoped. Not only did the bridge open on schedule, but Eiffel gained a reputation as an innovative and efficient engineer. The project established the procedure by which Eiffel worked for the rest of his life. Difficult technical problems presented a challenge to his keen analytical mind. To solve them, Eiffel broke new ground in technology, engineering, and construction.

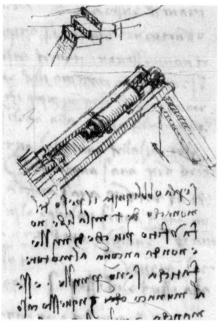

Illustration by Leonardo da Vinci of a pile driver. Eiffel introduced a new system of pile driving in 1858.

THE FAMILY MAN

By this time, Eiffel had matured into a hardworking, serious young man, a far cry from his days as a student. Although sometimes aloof and formal, he could also be quite charming. He was modest, so much so that any talk of his considerable technical skills and expertise left him flustered. He had never aspired to be a great man and had always looked forward to living life as simply as possible. His accomplishments sometimes brought him more notoriety than he wanted.

Although Eiffel's professional life was thriving, he led a reclusive personal life. He had few friends in Paris and spent much of his time working and studying. When it came to selecting a wife, Eiffel was somewhat less than romantic. In a letter to his mother, he described his ideal candidate. "What I need," he wrote, "is a good housekeeper who won't get on my nerves too much, who will be as faithful as possible, and who will give me fine children."[16] A business acquaintance of Eiffel's father in Dijon suggested that a meeting between Eiffel and his granddaughter, Marie Gaudelet, might be in order. Eiffel had, in fact, known Marie since childhood. She must have met at least some of his criteria because he married her in 1862.

The couple moved permanently to Paris, where Eiffel found a comfortable apartment for them. During the next fifteen years, the Eiffel's home resounded with the laughter of the five children they had together. But in 1877 Marie fell seriously ill with pneumonia and died. Eiffel was devastated and never married again.

OUT ON HIS OWN

In 1864, Eiffel left the General Railway Company to go into business for himself as the proprietor of G. Eiffel et Compagnie. Later he changed the name of his business to the Compagnie des Établissements Eiffel, after he formed a partnership with another engineer, Théophile Seyrig. One of his first jobs as an independent entrepreneur found Eiffel traveling to Egypt to deliver a shipment of locomotives. Always interested in seeing other engineering and technological projects, Eiffel made a point of visiting the newly opened Suez Canal and took careful note of the canal technology.

By 1876, Eiffel had opened a series of metalworking shops in the industrial suburb of Levallois-Perret, located to the northwest

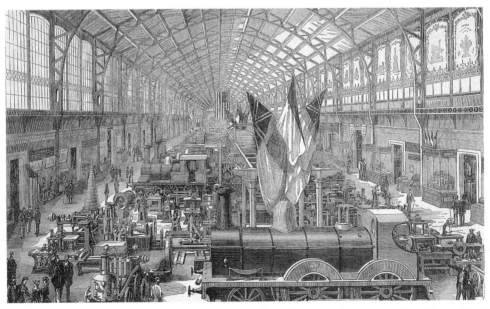

Eiffel worked on the design for iron arch girders and support beams for Machinery Hall (pictured) at the 1878 Paris Universal Exhibition.

of Paris. That year also saw Eiffel hard at work on a design for some iron arch-girders, or curved iron support beams, that were to be used in the construction of the entrance hall for the Palais des Machines (Machinery Hall), one of the featured exhibition buildings for the 1878 Paris Universal Exposition. Projected as one of the largest buildings ever built for an exposition, Machinery Hall was to be constructed in the shape of a rectangle measuring 1,608 feet by 1,266 feet. The arches Eiffel had been commissioned to design extended the building's length by 82 feet.

In his design for the arches, Eiffel decided not to use the traditional form of iron construction but instead chose wrought iron, a special type of iron made with a small amount of carbon. This combination made for a building material that was easier to bend. Eiffel labored to come up with a formula that would guarantee the arches were both strong and flexible. His efforts proved successful. He developed a method that created sturdy but lightweight trusses, or frameworks, and arches. His technique, which produced a webbed appearance in his structures, became Eiffel's trademark. Not only were his structures interesting to look at, but they could withstand the elements, especially high winds. His innovative use of wrought iron signaled what one architectural historian described as the "architecture of the future, light, aerial, open to sunlight, an architecture of voids rather than solids."[17]

A NEW KIND OF CONSTRUCTION

As news of his reputation spread, Eiffel found himself hired to undertake larger and more lucrative projects. His company was called upon to supply the metal framework for such buildings as exhibition halls, train stations, and churches. Yet Eiffel's specialty remained the construction of bridges. Between 1867 and 1885, Eiffel's company constructed forty-two railway bridges and viaducts. One of his first big projects came with the design of the Sioule Bridge, which spanned the Sioule River north of Clermont-Ferrand, a major commercial and manufacturing city located in south-central France. Completed in 1869, the bridge stood 262 feet above the river, making it one of the highest bridges in the world at that time.

The project was important for Eiffel for it enabled him to try out three important innovations that he would later use on almost every project he undertook, including the Eiffel Tower. For the first time, Eiffel eliminated the use of the regular, heavy, and brittle iron that had been the standard material in bridge construction. Instead, he again relied on wrought iron, which he found to be stronger, more flexible, and, when used in bridge trusses, better able to resist strong winds. Eiffel also decided to curve the edges of the piers—often square or rectangular in shape—to carry the weight of a structure. By curving the piers, Eiffel made them more durable and stable as a base. Finally, he introduced a new method known as launching. Rollers, metal cylinders mounted on top of a rocker, that consisted of large flat pieces of metal that rocked back and forth, allowed each individual piece of the bridge to be moved more easily into place. The effect was not unlike a large seesaw moving across the length of the bridge rocking and rolling each piece of the bridge into place. This innovative method also helped to support each individual bridge piece more evenly as it was being connected to the piers.

Eiffel's company also took more construction jobs outside of France. He built a bridge for the Portuguese national railway that spanned the Douro River, located near the city of Oporto. Because the river was deep, Eiffel determined that the traditional technique of installing a central pier to support the main portion of the bridge would not work. Instead, to cross the 525-foot-wide river, he designed a trussed parabolic arch. This curved arch, which was made up of a series of crisscrossed beams, supported the central span of the bridge. The arch's sides were set oblique (angles set at less than 90 degrees or more than 180 degrees) to each other to offer resistance to the wind.

The arch at Oporto was the largest ever attempted at that time. Because no scaffolding could be erected in the center of the river, Eiffel's construction crews built the arch in two halves. Each half was supported from above by steel cables attached to stone piers on the banks. As the work progressed, more cables were added as needed. Eventually the two halves met 200 feet above the center of the river. The finished bridge, completed in 1876, was widely recognized as one of the most masterful engineering feats of the time.

BUILDING THE GARABIT BRIDGE

Not to be outdone, a French railway company contacted Eiffel in 1879 about building a bridge above the Truyere River near

Some of Eiffel's most important work was bridge construction like this one in Oporto, Portugal.

Garabit, in southern France. This was no ordinary request. The company proposed building a bridge that would stand 400 feet above the Truyere River.

When the company presented its proposal, Eiffel responded with a plan similar to the bridge design he had completed at Oporto. Still, the Garabit Bridge, in the end, dwarfed the Oporto structure. The projected bridge would stand 400 feet high and 1,850 feet long. The deck of the bridge would be supported by five metal piers and a great parabolic arch with a span of 541 feet. The proposed project would require 3,587 tons of wrought iron and was estimated to cost $627,400. When completed, it would be the highest arched bridge in the world

In June 1879 Eiffel received permission from the Ministry of Roads and Bridges to begin work. Given his success at Oporto, the ministry was convinced that if any engineer could complete the project, it was Gustave Eiffel. The office even went so far as

ONE SMALL INCIDENT

Only a single incident upset Eiffel's careful calculations in the construction of his first big bridge project. One afternoon, a worker fell from the scaffolding into the waters of the Garonne. Caught in the current, the man seemed sure to drown. Seeing what had happened, Eiffel removed his shoes and his vest and jumped into the water, bringing the man safely ashore. Ever the gentleman, Eiffel, while drying off and dressing himself, cautioned the workers to be more careful in the future. As a token of appreciation for saving their comrade's life, the workers chipped in to have a medal made that depicted the bridge and the innovative pile driver that Eiffel had used for its construction.

to state that, "M[onsieur] Eiffel is the only person with such experience, since it is he who invented the means of stiffening piers and bridge deck against wind action."[18]

To make sure that construction went as smoothly as possible, Eiffel applied his trademark precision to every aspect of the work. He made careful notes about how much stress the metal trusses could withstand both when idle and in use. He studied in detail the effect of temperature changes on all the components of the bridge. Eiffel wanted to make sure that the bridge would be as sturdy and as safe as possible.

The Garabit Bridge took five years to complete. When finished, the structure was hailed as one of the greatest engineering feats in history, as well as one of Eiffel's finest works. In November 1884 the first train pulling twenty-two cars lumbered over the bridge without incident.

THE MASTER BUILDER

By the beginning of the 1880s, Gustave Eiffel was recognized as one of the finest engineers and builders of his age. Making the most of the new technological advances, Eiffel and his company went on to accomplish a number of important building projects that took him all over the world. The projects were as diverse as the technical problems they presented. One of Eiffel's most famous undertakings, the Viana Bridge in Portugal, was a combined road and railway bridge. Completed in 1877, the bridge was one of the longest ever built, spanning 2,414 feet and resting on nine piers. The deck, or road, alone weighed 1,764 tons.

In Hungary, Eiffel designed the Pest train station, also built in 1877. This ornate building encompassed 140,000 square feet and was one of the first examples of Art Nouveau, an elaborate architectural style known for its decorative metal components. In his own country, Eiffel constructed the Dome of the Nice Observatory, completed in 1885. He built the iron framework and the exterior that covered the 74-foot dome, which was the largest of its day.

Eiffel also undertook projects outside of Europe. The Tan An Bridge in Cochin, China was one of the many commissions he accepted in Asia. The Tan An was similar to some of Eiffel's earlier bridges in that he faced once again the challenge of building over a deep river. In this case, the 262-foot bridge was built in two sections. Then each section was pushed toward the other until they met and joined above the river. Eiffel repeatedly used this method, known as bootstrapping, to build bridges across especially deep rivers and gorges.

Eiffel was also responsible for the creation of prefabricated campaign bridges for the military of different nations. These bridges were constructed of a small number of standardized parts and could be dismantled, transported, and reassembled.

THE TAY BRIDGE DISASTER

When preparing his later bridge designs, Gustave Eiffel no doubt had the Tay Bridge in mind. Built in Scotland in 1878, the Tay Bridge was the scene of a horrific accident. Constructed of wrought iron, the bridge was one of the largest and best-known engineering marvels of the late nineteenth century. It was designed by the noted British engineer Sir Thomas Bouch. Unfortunately, Bouch badly miscalculated certain factors such as the wind load, or the forces that would be exerted on the bridge by the wind. One December evening strong winds swirled around the bridge. As an eight-car train carrying seventy-five passengers was crossing, thirteen of the bridge's eighty-five spans gave way, spilling the train and its occupants into the water below. No one survived.

The French army was the first to make use of these mobile bridges, which were sturdy enough to accommodate even the heaviest equipment and artillery. Later, the Russian, Austro-Hungarian, and Italian armies also adopted Eiffel's design.

No project was deemed impossible for Eiffel. He constructed gasworks (factories that produced gas for the purpose of lighting), covered markets, the famous Bon Marché department store in Paris, iron framing for the cathedral of Notre-Dame, and, of course, his specialty, bridges and train stations located throughout Asia, South America, and Europe.

THE STATUE OF LIBERTY

For several years, Parisians murmured about one amazing project that had been under way since 1875. To help the United States celebrate its own Centennial Exposition, which was to be held in Philadelphia in 1876, and as a token of the continuing goodwill and friendship of the French toward the Americans, French statesman Édouard-René Lefebvre suggested that France present the United States with a special gift: a statue depicting Liberty. Lefebvre hired noted sculptor Frédéric-Auguste Bartholdi to undertake the work while he set about raising funds for the project.

The plaster model of the proposed statue, *Liberty Enlightening the World*, was a wonderful sight. Bartholdi created a beautiful and stately statue of a woman with a crown, standing straight and holding a raised torch in her right hand. The problem, though, was how to translate the model into a finished statue. The proposed sculpture would be the largest ever raised, measuring 151 feet high. The head alone would extend 17 feet from chin to crown; the index finger on the left hand would be 8 feet long. The arm holding the torch would extend 42 feet and would be 12 feet thick. Lady Liberty, if successfully executed, would be a colossal masterpiece.

But a trickier problem confronted Bartholdi. He faced the dilemma of how best to construct the statue so it could be disassembled for transport to New York. Then there was the problem of how to stabilize the statue so that it could withstand the raging Atlantic winds that gusted through New York City harbor. Enter Gustave Eiffel. Bartholdi sought Eiffel's help in devising a solution to these problems and Eiffel was more than happy to take on the challenge.

To accommodate the dimensions of the statue, Eiffel proposed the construction of an iron skeleton frame to which sheets of metal could then be attached. He embedded vertical steel beams in the granite base of the statue to which thin sheets of copper were attached. This procedure, Eiffel thought, would result in a lighter but stronger statue, a structure fully capable of bearing enormous weight and enduring the elements.

By the spring of 1883, Parisians gathered to watch workmen attach three hundred sheets of copper to the statue's iron frame. Finally completed in early 1884, Lady Liberty was disassembled, packed, and sent to her permanent home in New York City. Once again, Eiffel had come to the rescue, solving a perplexing set of technical problems.

By 1887, his colleagues recognized Eiffel as unquestionably one of the greatest construction engineers of the time. He had demonstrated again and again the ability to decipher the most complex and stubborn technical problems and often embraced innovative techniques that no one had tried or even dared to consider. Yet, for all his many accomplishments, few outside of the engineering profession had ever

Eiffel designed the weight-bearing vertical steel beams imbedded in the base of the Statue of Liberty.

heard of him. With his entry into the Centennial Exposition Competition of 1887, all that changed. The winning design ultimately made Gustave Eiffel a household name, and the tower he built an enduring symbol of France.

A WORK IN PROGRESS

At the time Gustave Eiffel won the Exposition competition, he was fifty-five years old. He had established a reputation for the construction of bridges and buildings that were sturdy, reliable, and innovative. He was known for his intellectual precision, his careful attention to detail, and his unflappable personality. If anything bothered him, it was inefficiency in the design and execution of a project.

AN ORIGINAL MASTERPIECE

In arguing for his tower design, Eiffel told the members of the Exposition Committee that in order to illustrate the progress of French technology, the structure would need to be built of new materials and employ new building techniques. Therefore, he first had to decide whether wrought iron, cast iron, or steel was the best material to use. Wrought iron was heaviest and least likely to buckle. It was also easier to work with than cast iron or steel, and more capable of withstanding the elements. Cast iron tended to be brittle and was not nearly as strong as steel or wrought iron. Steel was lighter than iron but might not prove strong enough to support the weight of the tower or be able to stand up against the elements, especially high winds. Steel was also more expensive, since it was still a fairly new material. In the end, Eiffel, who was by this time an expert on the characteristics of various metals, determined that the tower should be built of wrought iron, the only available material which combined strength, flexibility, and durability with reasonable costs.

The biggest problem that Eiffel struggled with in his design was how to protect the tower from the wind. Using the lattice beams that graced his viaducts and bridges would not work here. Instead a new design would have to be developed. In the end, he proposed erecting a series of lattice-trussed piers with incurving edges. This would not only cut down on wind resistance—the piers with their curving design would be more aerodynamic—but also, in theory, these specially designed supports would hold up a tower of any height and weight. All that remained, of course, was for Eiffel to put the theory into practice to see if it worked.

As Eiffel envisioned it, the tower was to rest on a foundation of four large stone piers. On top of these, four wrought-iron legs would rest. The final design also called for a 4,200-square-meter (45,200-square-foot) gallery (a seating area) to occupy the first level, a 900-square-meter (9,700-square-foot) gallery on the second level, and, on the third level, a 250-square-meter (2,700-square-foot) dome surrounded by an outside balcony. Not only would this area provide a spectacular view of the Paris skyline, but according to the practical Eiffel it would be used to conduct scientific experiments.

Getting Under Way

Eiffel was confident that the project would succeed. He had worked hard at his calculations, insuring that every metal beam, every bolt, and every hole would be as precise as possible. Others, however, were more skeptical. What Eiffel proposed had

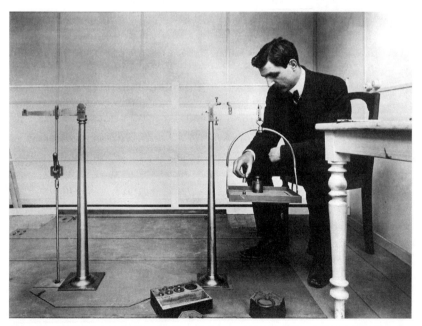

Gustave Eiffel (pictured) calculated the precise weight and balance for the construction of the tower.

never been attempted before, let alone accomplished. His design had no precedent, and many suspected that what looked feasible on paper might not work in practice. The size of the masonry bases that were to support the tower were, by themselves, twice as large as anything Eiffel had ever tried to build. Critics further pointed out that almost every piece of the tower would have to be designed separately to make sure the measurements were accurate to within one-tenth of a millimeter, or less than four-one-thousandths of an inch. This level of precision seemed impossible to achieve or sustain.

To complicate matters even further, the timetable for completion of the project was growing rapidly shorter. By the time the committee approved the design for the Eiffel Tower, as the structure was to be known, Eiffel had only a little more than two years to finish the project for the opening of the exposition in the spring of 1889. The Washington Monument, not nearly so extensive an enterprise, had taken more than thirty-six years to complete (although the outbreak of the Civil War did interrupt the work). Pessimists wondered if Eiffel could construct in two years a tower nearly twice that size.

WHERE TO BUILD?

Then there was the problem with the tower's proposed location. The competition guidelines specified that the winning design be constructed in the Champ de Mars. After approving the design, however, some members of the committee began to have second thoughts about where the tower ought to be situated. They wondered whether such a large tower would spoil the natural vistas and symmetrical proportions of the Champ de Mars. One committee member questioned the desirability of "construct[ing] the tower in the bottom of the Seine valley. Would it not be better to place it in an elevated position, on a rise which would be a sort of pedestal for it and make it stand out more?"[19] Others worried that the tower would dwarf the magnificent palaces already located in and around the park. Still others became concerned that if the tower were built in the park, its presence would inhibit future exhibits and activities at the location.

Those committee members who defended building the Eiffel Tower in the Champ de Mars suggested that moving it far from the center of the exhibition would seriously compromise the financial benefits it was expected to provide. There was no doubt

THE CONTRACT

Gustave Eiffel's contract with the city of Paris was a carefully worded agreement. The sixteen-page document clearly spelled out a number of issues, including the financing of, and time limit for, construction of the tower, and who was ultimately responsible for its maintenance. City officials requested that at least one room on every level of the tower be used for scientific observations and experiments, a stipulation to which Eiffel was more than happy to agree. In fact, he himself had insisted upon it. Furthermore, Eiffel, rather than his company, took sole responsibility for the project. This meant that he personally bore the costs for much of the tower construction.

To secure financing, Eiffel created another company that consisted of a group of three banks, in which he owned the majority share. Any profits made from the tower during the exposition, therefore, automatically belonged to him. The city of Paris also agreed to grant Eiffel the authorization for operation of the tower after the exhibition had closed. In this way, Eiffel became sole owner of the tower and received any income from the use of the tower for a period of twenty years. This arrangement proved extremely profitable to him because he opened a restaurant in the tower. After twenty years, ownership of the tower reverted to the city of Paris, which continues to own it today.

that the Eiffel Tower would be the main attraction of the exposition; therefore its location was critical to the overall success of the entire endeavor.

With these conflicting opinions in mind, the committee reviewed its options and reaffirmed its original choice. The tower would be erected in the Champ de Mars. According to one of the drawings the committee used, the Eiffel Tower, as described by Alfred Picard, the official historian of the exposition, was to be situated "approximately halfway between the Trocadéro dome and the cupola of the Palace of Various Industries, towards the upper part of the old city gardens and far enough from the Seine [River]."[20] This location saved money in two ways. First, the ground around the Trocadéro had been the site of extensive excavations. If the tower were to be built here, the

The Eiffel Tower was erected on the Champ de Mars (pictured).

city would have to build more substantial foundations for the tower, which would mean more money. Second, with its monumental archways the tower could function as an entranceway to the exposition, thereby saving the cost of constructing a separate one.

With the committee now in agreement about the location of the tower, Eiffel started to work in earnest on January 1, 1887. While awaiting the decision about the final location of the tower, however, Eiffel had not wasted any time. Instead, while the committee members debated, he had made several important changes to the original design. He scaled down the first-level glass-walled hall and removed the ornate metal decorations that would have added color to the tower. Eiffel also altered the shape of the four gigantic arches at the base. These modifications, in the end, would give the tower a lighter, almost floating appearance. Declaring that the tower would "raise to the glory of modern science, and to the greater honor of French industry, an arch of triumph,"[21] Eiffel never doubted the importance of the undertaking, and knew the tower would generate enthusiasm. Little did he suspect that it would also bring great controversy as well.

"THE ODIOUS COLUMN OF BOLTED METAL"

As if dealing with the exposition committee had not been trying enough, Eiffel now faced another potential crisis. For months, many Parisians had wondered whether the tower would become a reality at all. Once excavation began in 1887, though, that skepticism turned first to shock and then to anger. In February, a group of forty-seven self-appointed cultural critics, including poets, artists, sculptors, and writers, banded together to stop construction of the tower. The members of the group included some of the leading figures in French cultural life, including writers Alexandre Dumas and Guy de Maupassant, artists Ernest Meissonier and Adolphe-William Bouguereau. Also among the critics was the noted French architect Charles Garnier, who had designed the Paris opera house.

Garnier in particular was extremely upset with the design of the tower. He found the use of the new experimental materials such as wrought and cast iron distasteful. If anything, Garnier feared that science as symbolized by Eiffel and his tower would overshadow the true art of architecture. For Garnier, structures like Eiffel's were anything but artistic. Commenting on another building that employed the use of an exposed metal exterior, Garnier stated that the building was "an example of

A FAMOUS CRITIC

One of the most vocal critics of the Eiffel Tower was writer Guy de Maupassant. Despite the ridicule the "Artists' Protest" received, Maupassant never altered his objections to the tower. According to one unverified story often told throughout Paris, Maupassant often lunched at the tower's second-level restaurant because, he said, it was the only place in Paris where he did not have to look at the tower. Maupassant even wrote about the tower in one of his stories, "La Vie Errante" ("The Errant Life"), quoted here from Joseph Harriss's book, *The Tallest Tower*. Maupassant describes the tower as a "tall, skinny pyramid of iron ladders, this giant and disgraceful skeleton . . . which aborts into the thin ridiculous profile of a factory chimney." Later on, Maupassant would always declare that the reason he left France was to get away from the Eiffel Tower.

Writer Guy de Maupassant was an ardent critic of the Eiffel Tower.

the bad effect produced by iron when it is used tastelessly and with the pretension [idea] of replacing stone."[22]

In the end, concerned that it would destroy the beauty of the Paris skyline, the group sent a letter of protest to the Minister of Public Works, Charles Adophe Alphand, whose department was ultimately responsible for the exposition. Known as the "Artists' Protest" the letter stated in part: "We come to protest with all our strength, with all our indignation, in the name of betrayed French taste . . . against the erection in the heart of our capital of the useless and monstrous Eiffel Tower."[23]

As far as the opponents of the tower were concerned there was nothing spectacular or even attractive about it. In the letter, they referred to the tower variously as a "black and gigantic factory chimney . . . , [a] barbarous mass . . . , [and an] odious [detestable] column of bolted metal."[24] Nothing short of canceling the tower's construction would do. Completion of the tower, the critics resolved, would not only destroy a beautiful city but would make Paris and its inhabitants the laughingstock of the entire world.

Upon receiving the letter, Alphand turned it over to Édouard Lockroy, whose idea it had been to build a tower in the first place. Lockroy immediately responded to Alphand by saying:

> One can tell from the signatures [that] this protest is the result of collaboration of the most famous writers and poets of our time. . . . [But] the protest is already irrelevant. You will inform the senders that construction of the tower was decided upon a year ago and that the work site has been open for a month. They could have protested in time; they did not, and "honorable" indignation unfortunately comes a bit late.[25]

Lockroy's response was later printed in the Paris newspapers. Instead of gaining support, Eiffel's adversaries found themselves the objects of ridicule as city residents read with great delight a reprinting of Lockroy's letter. As much as the artists disliked the tower, they hated being made fun of even more. As a result, their protest quietly faded away.

In an ironic turn of events, several of those who had initially opposed construction of the tower visited it during the exhibition, and, instead of condemning the structure, came to admire and praise Eiffel's work. For instance, French composer Charles

Gounod would in fact compose some musical pieces as a tribute to the tower, as well as entertaining guests at a small private party hosted by Eiffel at his private apartment after the tower's opening.

One of the tower's most vocal critics, however, the architect Charles Garnier, never wavered in his belief that the tower was nothing more than a pile of scrap metal. Despite these criticisms, in the end it would be Garnier's architectural philosophy that would be called worn and outdated, as Eiffel's tower was hailed as pointing architecture in a new direction.

ANSWERING TO CRITICS

For his part, Eiffel did not let the controversy pass quietly. Instead, he responded to his detractors. This was in itself highly unusual. In the late nineteenth century, engineers were often thought of as little more than fancy mechanics who had little education. No one believed they had

The architect of the Paris Opera House, Charles Garnier (pictured), joined other artists to protest the construction of the Eiffel Tower.

any sense of beauty. It was inconceivable to French cultural leaders that an engineer would even understand why the artists were upset about the tower in the first place.

But Eiffel was different. He had passed through the strict and tough French school system. On top of that, he was a college graduate, with a diploma from one of Europe's first great engineering schools. Eiffel was a thoughtful man who had in the course of designing his tower, tackled the difficult questions of combining both taste and technology to create something that most would find pleasing.

When asked for an interview by the Paris newspaper *Le Temps*, Eiffel was happy to oblige. One of the first things he addressed was the timing of the artists' protest. In fact, Eiffel was quite puzzled that anyone had chosen to protest the tower so late—almost two years after the design and plan for the tower had been first submitted. Eiffel also pointed out that as one of the members of the Tower Commission, Charles Garnier had raised no objections to the tower design in those early stages. As Eiffel pointed out, "He [Garnier] did nothing to show that he did not approve of it, so he is protesting against himself."[26] Besides, the ground had been broken and materials were being prepared.

When the reporter asked Eiffel if he thought engineers could create beautiful structures at all, Eiffel replied:

> Is it because we are engineers that we do not pay attention to beauty? Do not the laws of natural forces always conform to the secret laws of harmony? . . . Now what condition do I have to take in to consideration above all others in a tower? Wind resistance. Well, I maintain that the curves of the four arrises [arches] of the monument, as the calculations have determined them, will give an impression of beauty because they will demonstrate to the viewer the boldness of the conception.

"REAPING LIGHTNING IN THE CLOUDS"

One critic who eventually changed his mind about the tower was the writer and composer Émile Goudeau. Although he had been one of the forty-seven detractors who signed the petition denouncing the tower, Goudeau gradually came to appreciate the structure and even became good friends with Eiffel himself. In his book, *Gustave Eiffel*, Henri Loyette prints one of Goudeau's most vivid descriptions of the tower as it was being built.

> A thick smoke of coal and tar caught in our throats and we were deafened by the sound of iron roaring under the hammer. [On the second platform] they were fixing bolts; workmen perched in a seat a few centimeters wide, struck the bolts in rotation with their iron hammers. One would have said they were [black]smiths quietly absorbed in striking some rhythmical blows on the anvil in some village forge; only they were not hitting downwards, vertically, but horizontally and as sparks flew out at each blow, these blackened men, magnified by the perspective of the open sky, looked as if they were reaping lightning in the clouds.

Eiffel went on to state that he believed the tower will have its own beauty. . . . Up to now it has only been known by an elevation drawing; yet even though hundreds of thousands of copies have been made of it, is it possible to grasp the overall artistic effect of a monument from a single drawing?"[27]

Eiffel also answered critics who claimed that the tower would overshadow the other cultural and architectural attractions of the city. He made it clear that he did not agree and said the tower was itself an expression of French culture, an example of both French technical expertise and French aesthetic sensibility. He explained his plans to use part of the tower as a laboratory in which to conduct experiments in astronomy, meteorology, and physics. These future findings, Eiffel believed, would be both important and helpful in learning about the world.

In closing, Eiffel contended that construction of the tower was important not only for Paris but for all of France. If France were to be taken seriously by other industrial nations, then the Eiffel Tower would go a long way toward silencing foreign critics of French progress. Eiffel stated, "It seems to me that the Eiffel Tower is worthy of being treated with respect, if only because it will show that we [the French] are . . . the country of engineers and builders who are called upon all over the world to construct bridges, viaducts, train stations, and the great monuments of modern industry."[28]

Having defended his reputation, his profession, and his tower, Eiffel turned his attention back to his work. There was little time now to waste on tiresome distractions. He had a tower to build.

A Dizzily Ridiculous Tower

After months of jousting with the committee, answering his critics, and explaining his intentions, Gustave Eiffel was at last
ready to begin building the tower. Before construction could get
under way, however, Eiffel ordered soil samples taken so that he
had a thorough knowledge of the land on which he was to build
before he started work. When he received the findings, Eiffel
had to confront yet another complication. The land to the south
and east of the construction site consisted of clay covered with a
thick layer of gravel. The firm composition of this soil perfectly
suited Eiffel's purposes. To the north and west, though, Eiffel
learned that the soil was mostly wet sand, clay, and mud mixed
with an assortment of rotting wood, pottery fragments, pieces of
masonry, and animal bones. This soft, mucky soil was less than
an ideal base in which to install the foundations of the mammoth tower. To make matters worse, this low-lying area faced
the constant threat of flooding since it was so close to the Seine.

Eiffel considered how to overcome this troublesome problem. He decided to use two different systems to set the foundation piers supporting the tower. For the south and east, he
utilized a dry foundation system. To the north and west, in the
area closest to the Seine, he constructed a compressed air system similar to those he had used in erecting railroad bridges
over rivers. Eiffel believed that if workers dug the riverside
foundations sixteen feet deeper than the dry-side foundations,
the piers would rest on the more solid and durable clay that lay
beneath the soft, moist soil near the riverbed. If his calculations
were correct, the piers would then be secure and stable enough
to support the weight of the tower.

A New Kind Of Construction

To sink the riverside foundations as deeply as he thought they
needed to go, Eiffel decided to use caissons, watertight chambers

most often used in underwater construction. He had had considerable experience with caissons on a number of his bridge projects. On January 26, 1887, workmen began the difficult task of excavating the land so that the caissons could be installed. By late March, Eiffel's metal shops were at work producing these containers, which enabled workers to dig underground, beneath the water level of the Seine. Fashioned from sheet metal and measuring fifty feet in length, twenty feet in width, and ten feet in depth, each of the sixteen caissons that Eiffel used (four for each foundation leg) was like an underground room. Entering the caissons through an air lock located at the top, workmen descended a ladder until they arrived at the chamber. Once inside the caissons, they used pickaxes and shovels to break up the soil that the caisson itself had loosened. The workers then hoisted the dirt to the surface in buckets.

The wedge-shaped walls at the bottom of the caissons formed cutting edges that bored through the earth. As workmen removed the soil, the caissons, which weighed approximately thirty-four tons each, sunk deeper into the earth, displacing even more soil, rocks, and other debris, which workmen also removed. Relying on this innovative technique, Eiffel found a way to bypass the soft, wet, sandy soil and rest the foundations of the tower on the harder, more solid clay underneath.

When the workers had completed the excavations, Eiffel ordered them to prepare the foundations. Each of the tower's

Foundations supporting the Eiffel Tower were sunk deeply into the earth at an angle to provide stability.

piers had been designed to rest on a massive pile of cement and stone. These piles were set at an angle so that the curving columns bearing the tower's weight would be positioned at a more stable angle. Next Eiffel had the workmen pour twenty feet of quick-drying cement into each hole to act as a base for the foundation piers. On top of this, Eiffel added gigantic blocks of limestone extracted from the famous Souppes-sur-Loing quarry in France. Capping the limestone blocks were two layers of cut stone from the Château Landon quarry, located to the southeast of Paris, which had provided the stone for two other celebrated Parisian monuments, the Arc de Triomphe and the Sacré Coeur basilica. Two large steel anchor bolts were used to further secure each foundation block. The bolts, each measuring twenty-six feet long and four inches in diameter, were attached to an iron base called a shoe. The bolts were then embedded into the center of each stone. Theoretically, the bolts were not necessary to add strength and stability because Eiffel had designed the tower so that its own weight guaranteed that it would not topple over. But he left nothing to chance.

To insure that the foundation stones would stay put, Eiffel invented an interesting device. Located in the hollow of each shoe, he placed a piston that could be moved by water released under pressure. This technique was truly innovative, for these pistons, acting as hydraulic jacks, could raise or lower each of the sixteen caissons, almost guaranteeing that the piers would remain perfectly horizontal when the tower's first-level iron horizontal beams, or girders, were installed. Eiffel's innovations ensured that the tower would be in perfect alignment. Precision and innovation were once again his guiding principles of construction.

THE FIRST STAGE

By the end of June 1887, Eiffel had the foundation completely in place. During the first five months of work, approximately 25 acres of earth had been excavated and the 180-foot piers consisting of some 16,000 cubic yards of masonry had been set. By July 1, 1887, the tower began to rise above the rooftops of Paris.

Eiffel implemented a rigid construction schedule. He had each piece of the tower fashioned separately so that every hole for the 2.5 million bolts, or special pins called rivets, needed to

BEHIND THE SCENES

Although the attention of the press and the public centered around the activity taking place in the Champ de Mars, there was plenty going on at Gustave Eiffel's shops as well. To prepare to build the tower, Eiffel and his assistants made more than 1,700 general drawings. To make sure that not a single rivet was out of place, Eiffel's technicians produced an additional 5,329 mechanical drawings depicting 18,038 different parts of the tower, leaving no doubt about the exact placement of every bolt and girder or structural support. These drawings required the work of thirty draftsmen and took eighteen months to produce.

This extensive attention to detail was unheard of in nineteenth-century engineering. More often than not, workers received semifinished pieces at the site. Engineers then consulted the blueprints and added the necessary finishing touches before the workmen put the pieces in place. With Eiffel's system, there was no need for any last-minute checking. His twenty riveting teams, for instance, had only to line up the holes that had already been punched into the girders and go to work. On average, they drove 1,650 rivets a day during the construction of the tower. With this system, Eiffel set new standards for accuracy in design and speed of construction.

Eiffel's bolt and riveting system set new, higher architectural standards.

put the tower together could be drilled at precisely the right spot. This procedure enabled Eiffel to achieve an unprecedented level of accuracy in construction. Two-thirds of the rivet holes were drilled while the pieces were still in the shop. When the pieces arrived at the site, workers drilled in the remaining holes. This way all the holes were placed accurately.

Each day, spectators watched as finished iron pieces arrived by horse-drawn wagons from Eiffel's shops in Levallois-Perret, located three miles away. During the course of the construction, the shops produced more than 400 tons of girders, beams, and trusses every month. Once the pieces arrived at the site, workmen hoisted them into position by means of steam-powered cranes.

When it came to the size of the tower's materials, Eiffel again broke all the rules. He wanted no piece used in the construction to weigh more than three tons, making for comparatively light individual components. From his earlier experiences, Eiffel learned that using smaller, lighter components made the work easier, faster, and safer. Of course, the smaller the individual pieces the more of them Eiffel needed to complete the tower. But the chance for accidents also diminished considerably because the smaller, lighter pieces were easier for workmen to handle.

Given the nature of the project, Eiffel managed with a work crew that was really quite small, never numbering more than 250 at any one time. Of that number, about 199 were full-time employees of Eiffel's company. The remaining workers were hired as needed. So few workers building such a giant tower gave the impression, as one architectural historian wrote, "that the tower was constructing itself. . . . It was a smooth, well-oiled operation where human participation seemed limited, almost nonexistent."[29]

Eiffel managed to build the tower with a relatively small number of workers.

The Creeper Cranes

The tower frame slowly began taking shape. As column after column moved into place, Eiffel implemented yet another unconventional technique. On the sloping tracks inside the piers that would later be used to support elevators, Eiffel installed a series of cranes whose arms would lift construction materials from the ground and transport them to the tower's higher platforms. These remarkable machines, called creeper cranes, could pivot a full 360 degrees and could be moved up the tracks as construction progressed. The creeper cranes were the key components of Eiffel's construction system; without them, there was no way the tower could have been completed, as it would have been almost impossible to move materials up and down such great heights.

The creeper cranes delighted the sightseers who watched the tower's progress. One impressed newspaper reporter described their operation, writing, "It is curious and interesting to watch these four lifting machines climbing ever higher along with the iron columns. They turn left, right, in, out, picking up the huge metal beams and placing them exactly where they are supposed to go."[30]

To some spectators, however, the work seemed exceedingly dangerous and haphazard. Vicomte de Vogüé, a frequent visitor to the site, described the view: "Cranes clung onto the uprights [vertical beams]; they clambered along the girders like crabs with enormous pincers; they took items from the ground and bore them away to distribute them up above, sending them flying off in every direction."[31]

Despite appearances though, there was nothing disorganized or random in the process. Eiffel and his associates had estimated as precisely as possible every adjustment and every movement of every piece.

Reaching for the Top

By October 10, 1887, the tower stood at 92 feet. So far, it had required ten tons of iron and ninety-eight-thousand rivets. Before the tower could go any higher, however, workers had to construct temporary bracing to provide additional support so the tower would not lean or fall over. Workers placed the bracing, which consisted of twelve wood frames called pylons, 90 feet tall, beneath the three interior columns, or vertical posts, located in each pier. Once the bracing was in place, workers added four platforms, 150 feet high and 82 feet long, in the outside center of every face, or side, of the tower. Each face joined to form a square frame that helped offset the unavoidable increasing inward weight and pressure that would occur as the piers rose to greater heights. The frame also supported the heavy iron girders and trusses when they were finally raised to unite the tower's piers at the first level.

AFRAID OF DISASTER

As it became apparent that the tower would be a reality, many citizens who lived close to the construction site started to worry that pieces of the tower would come crashing through the roofs of their homes. One resident became so upset at the thought that he sued the city of Paris to halt construction. With the lawsuit pending, construction was immediately suspended.

It was months before workmen could return to the site. Finally, desperate to get on with the job, Eiffel agreed to assume personally all liability for damages should something go wrong during construction. If the tower proved dangerous in any way, Eiffel would destroy it at his own expense.

Although no other incidents slowed or halted construction, many Parisians remained unconvinced that the tower could withstand high winds or the elements. Some predicted that it would collapse before reaching its projected height. Others thought the conduits, or pipes, from the tower's lightning rods (devices used to protect a building from lightning damage), buried in the Seine, would kill all the fish. Still others, like the editor of *The New York Times*, reported that the tower, because of its height, would alter weather patterns in Paris. Furthermore, the Paris newspaper *Le Matin* declared in one of its headlines that the tower was sinking and advised that construction be stopped and the structure be demolished.

Each face of the tower joined to form a square frame.

Despite the predictions of disaster, Eiffel pressed on. By March 15, 1888, with the first level complete, the tower stood at 180 feet. The tower in its un-finished form, however, reminded many Parisians of a huge, squat, ugly metal beast, not the graceful structure they had been promised. Eiffel had a different view. Relieved that the tower construction had gone so smoothly, he wrote, "Joined by the belt of girders, the piers formed a solid table with a wide base. The sight of it alone was enough to brush aside any fear of its overturning. We no longer had to worry about a major accident, and any minor ones that might occur now could not compromise completion of the structure."[32]

THE NEXT STEP

To prepare for the next phase of construction, Eiffel arranged for an additional crane to be installed on the first-level platform, its tracks laid around the platform's perimeter. As the crane hoisted the necessary building materials from the ground to the first level, workmen placed them in small wagons that also rolled on tracks. They pulled the loaded wagons to the four creeper cranes, which then hoisted the materials to workers on the next level.

By July 1888 the second level was complete, elevating the tower to a height of 380 feet. On July 14, 1888, Bastille Day, on which the French commemorate the Revolution of 1789, the tower was the scene of many festivities. During the afternoon, Eiffel held a banquet for members of the press and used the oc-casion to promote the tower. He addressed the reporters, saying:

> Judging by the interest that the tower seems to inspire both in France and abroad, I believe it is fair to say that we are showing the world that France continues to be the leader of progress and that she is realizing a project which has often been tried or dreamed of. . . . Construc-tion of this tower will be one of the landmarks of modern industry.[33]

EFFICIENT WORKERS

With only eight months left to complete his work, Eiffel pushed his workers and himself harder than ever. Through the hot sum-mer months, workers toiled at least twelve hours a day. (During the rest of the year they had frequently worked nine- or ten-hour days.) Yet Eiffel was still in a tight race against the calendar.

Eiffel continued to search for every means possible to ensure that construction proceeded rapidly and efficiently. No detail was too minute to escape his notice. He decided, for example, that the workers' lunch hours were costing them valuable time away from the job. Moreover, as the tower rose, it took workers longer to reach the ground to eat their lunches and longer to

THE WORKERS

In the construction of the Eiffel Tower, French working-men encountered some of the toughest conditions they had ever faced. Not only were they at work on what was to be the tallest structure in the world, but Gustave Eiffel required them to adapt to new technology and equipment, most of which had never been seen, let alone used.

Fear of heights (acrophobia) or the loss of balance (vertigo) were rarely problems for the workers. Nevertheless, the possibility of a fall was always present, and grew as the tower rose. The open design of the tower also presented problems, for there was little protection from the elements, especially the icy winter winds that froze fingers to the metal and cooled hot rivets before they could be used.

The men in Eiffel's employ worked long hours to meet the construction deadline. They were, however, well paid by the standards of the day. At the outset of the project, wages ran from eight cents an hour for unskilled laborers to fourteen cents an hour for such skilled workers as carpenters and riveters. In July 1888 workers received a raise of one cent an hour, with another one cent raise coming in September. For many workers, this gesture was still not enough. In December 1888 workers insisted on another wage increase. Not wanting to give in to the workers, Eiffel refused to meet their demands. He did, though, promise to pay a bonus of one hundred francs to all workers who stayed on the job until the tower was completed. Dissatisfied, some workers quit. Eiffel simply replaced them with workers whom he later described as equally competent as the previous ones. In appreciation for their efforts in completing the tower, Eiffel honored his workers with a special plaque attached to the tower listing the names of all 199 men who had stayed on to finish the project.

climb the tower to go back to work when they had finished. Since they had not yet installed elevators, workers also got tired climbing from the tower to the ground and from the ground to the tower.

To solve this problem, Eiffel ordered the construction of a canteen, or small restaurant, on the first level of the tower. With the construction of the new canteen, workers did not have to climb all the way to the ground to eat. Consequently, they did not waste as much time or get as tired. The canteen proved so successful and so popular with the workers that when the second platform was finished Eiffel had the canteen moved there.

Workers toiled nine- to twelve-hour days to complete construction of the tower on time.

A RACE AGAINST TIME

Despite Eiffel's efforts to keep construction moving ahead at a steady pace, time was still a factor. To finish the tower on schedule, Eiffel again had to alter his building methods. By July 1888 the tower had risen to the second level. Each level now consisted of four rectangular piers joined by horizontal girders built on top of one another. From the second level to the top, though, the four piers needed to converge on one point, creating a single vertical iron column. This presented an entirely new challenge for Eiffel in terms of how to finish the tower's construction successfully.

To get materials to workmen on this level, Eiffel could not rely on the four creeper cranes he had been using. In their place, he put new fifty-ton creeper cranes on the vertical beams that rose from the center of the tower. He situated the cranes back-to-back so that they balanced each other and so he could be sure that workers on all four sides of the tower could reach

THE OBSERVERS

There is an outstanding visual record of the construction of the Eiffel Tower. A complete photographic history follows the project from the initial groundbreaking to the final stages of construction. Among these amazing documents is a series of photographs taken from the same vantage point that shows the tower rising stage by stage. No doubt, the photographers sensed that they were witnessing an event of great historical importance and wished to preserve it for future generations.

There is also extensive literature that reports contemporaries' impressions of the tower. Certainly among the most compelling accounts was that of an observer who visited the tower's first platform just as work was being finished. His description, quoted here from Joseph Harriss's book, *The Tallest Tower*, was first published in *L'Exposition de Paris 1889 (The Paris Exposition of 1889)*:

> At this height the city already appears immobile. The silhouettes of passersby . . . are like little black spots of ink in the streets. Only the rippling Seine seems still alive. To the south there is a fine view of the Exposition grounds, with the glass roof of the Machinery Hall looking like a lake of molten lead. I peek through a crack in the wooden flooring and look straight down into the void. Far below, I can see very small ducks swimming in a half-frozen pond. A shiver runs down my spine at the thought of a possible fall. . . . Continuing up this staircase, the cold iron railing hurts my fingers . . . the wind buffets me and I am blinded by the driving sleet. . . . I grab the railing again and shield my face with my arm. . . . At the height of 900 feet there is a wind of only fifteen miles per hour, but it is enough to take my breath away. Workers here are placing a rivet. The great nail is taken red-hot from its portable forge, positioned in the hole and struck with heavy hammers in a shower of sparks. Below, Paris seems to be sinking into the night like some fabled city descending to the bottom of the sea.

them. To give additional support to the cranes, Eiffel added 30-by-12-foot iron frames, bolted to the central beams. He then had the cranes attached to the beams.

When the workmen finished a 30-foot stretch of the tower they repeated the process, attached the cranes to the next set of beams, and continued to build upward. Proceeding in this way, the construction of each 30-foot section only took about thirty hours. To speed the process along even more, Eiffel operated simultaneously four hoisting systems consisting of steam-powered winches, machines used to lift materials. Spectators were treated to the sight of the steam winch lifting the materials placed in its hooks and ropes, from the ground to the first level. From there, a second steam winch transported the materials to the second platform; they then passed to a third winch that Eiffel had installed on a platform 650 feet above the ground. The last winch brought the materials and prefabricated panels to the creeper cranes. The entire process of raising materials from ground level to the highest elevation took only about twenty minutes. People gazed in wonder at this amazing sight, but for Eiffel it was all in a day's work.

INSTALLING THE ELEVATORS

The last important part of the tower to be completed was the elevator system. It was also the only job that Eiffel had to subcontract. Because he had relatively little control over this aspect of construction, it left him more nervous and frustrated than any other.

One reason for this worry was that the elevator industry was still in the early stages of development. Although steam-powered elevators had come into operation as early as the 1860s, the more powerful hydraulic technology that Eiffel insisted on using was less than a decade old. For once, Eiffel had misgivings about technology; he worried that it might be too risky for this aspect of the tower. Yet he knew that installing elevators in the tower was an absolute necessity. Visitors might be willing to climb the 363 steps from the ground level to the first platform, but few would be willing to ascend the additional 381 steps to the second level. Another 927 steps led from the second level to the top of the tower. And even though this area would not be open to the public, an elevator was necessary in order for workers—including Eiffel himself—to have access. For people to enjoy and work in

Elevators installed in the tower utilized hydraulic technology.

the tower, therefore, a safe and efficient elevator system was indispensable.

Complicating the addition of the elevators were the angled legs of the tower. The elevator cars could not be housed in a simple vertical shaft. Instead, they would have to travel on curved tracks aligned at different angles. The elevators would also have to accommodate the large number of people who would visit the tower and would thus be in almost continual use. An adequate elevator system was not going to be good enough. For Eiffel, the elevators had to be the best that technology could supply.

To get what he wanted, Eiffel hired three different companies, each one assigned an individual task. The French company of Roux, Combaluzier, and Lepape installed elevators to run from the ground to the first level in the east and west pillars. In the north pillar an American elevator company, Otis Elevators, installed an elevator that went directly from ground level to the second level. A second Otis elevator, located in the south pillar, operated between the first and second levels. Finally, another French firm, the Edoux Company, built the elevator that ran between the second and third platforms. Although the use of three different companies with three different systems seemed uncharacteristically inefficient on Eiffel's part, the three companies cooperated with each other and with Eiffel. In the end, the arrangement worked well and accomplished the primary goal: the installation of reliable elevators.

MISSION ACCOMPLISHED

By early 1889, Eiffel at last began to breathe a little easier. It looked as if he would meet the deadline. All that remained was to put the finishing touches on the tower, and then it would be ready to receive the thousands of visitors coming to the exposition. On the first level, where Eiffel expected the majority of visitors to spend most of their time, he added a rectangular walkway, 930 feet long and 9 feet wide with nine decorative arches on either side. There, the public would receive its first grand view of the tower. People could also buy souvenirs and eat at one of the level's four restaurants, each of which offered a different type of cuisine.

The second platform housed the offices of the French newspaper *Le Figaro*, which planned to publish a special daily edition during the exposition. There was also room for a pub and a pastry shop.

The third level, octagonal in shape, was completely enclosed in glass to protect visitors from the elements. From this enclosure, a short spiral staircase led to a small apartment in which Gustave Eiffel would make his home. On the small balcony surrounding the platform were two powerful spotlights mounted on a small track. The lights could be moved to illuminate the different monuments located throughout Paris. Positioned at the very top of the tower was a electric beacon, or light, with a range of nearly 120 miles. Enclosed by a cylinder that contained prisms of red, white, and blue, the French national colors, the electric lamp was timed to flash every ninety seconds. Eight lightning rods, also attached near the top, protected the tower from being damaged by lightning.

When the construction workers had finished construction, Eiffel had the tower painted. Barbados bronze, a reddish brown paint, applied in gradually lighter shades from the bottom to the top, would, Eiffel hoped, make the tower seem even taller than it was.

3. 7 janvier 1888.

4. 27 avril 1888.

5. 19 juin 1888.

6. 19 juillet 1888.

Construction of the Eiffel Tower was completed in March 1889.

The tower stood 986-feet-high and was the tallest structure in the world at the time.

Then, incredibly, it was over. By the end of March 1889, nearly six weeks before the exposition was to open, the Eiffel Tower stood complete. Its final height was recorded at 300.51 meters or 986 feet, the tallest structure in the world at that time. Eiffel not only made his deadline, but kept construction costs under budget. The 7,799,401 francs ($1,505,675) price tag was 6 percent less than the $1.6 million allotted for the project. To add to the growing list of amazing accomplishments, only one fatality had occurred during the construction. A young worker, showing off for his girlfriend, fell from the first floor platform just as the bell sounded to end the workday.

The tower denounced as ridiculous, monstrous, and an eyesore now dominated the Paris skyline. With its construction, Eiffel had not only enhanced his own reputation but had also altered the development of technology, engineering, construction, and architecture.

"More Famous Than I Am"

Except for a few minor adjustments made to the elevators, the remarkable tower was finished. To the few visitors who were allowed early access to the tower, it was clear that Eiffel's creation was something both special and remarkable. But the biggest test still lay ahead. The event for which the tower had been built and the celebration of the tower itself were just about to get under way. Only then would Eiffel and the members of the Exposition Committee know whether or not the tower would be the success they had hoped for.

For the Honor of France

On the afternoon of Sunday, March 31, 1889, a dignified group of men made their way to the Eiffel Tower to attend a *fête intime du chantier*, or "work-site party," hosted by Eiffel himself. Those in attendance included the prime minister of France, members of the Paris Municipal Council, Eiffel's business partners, and the directors of the exposition. Meeting Eiffel at 1:30 P.M., many in the group struggled to keep up with him as he climbed the stairs of the tower seemingly without effort. Some became so winded that, upon reaching the first platform, they stopped, unable to go on.

Those who could keep up with Eiffel arrived at the top of the tower a little after 2:00 P.M. There Eiffel unfurled a French flag measuring fifteen-by-twenty-five feet. Attaching the flag to its pole, he hoisted it to the top of the tower where it could be seen for miles. To accompany the flag raising, fireworks were set off on the second platform. With toasts of champagne, Eiffel saluted the guests and many of the workers who had also assembled. In all, it proved to be an exciting and memorable dedication.

Only one incident threatened the otherwise perfect afternoon. Shortly after the ceremony ended, while the guests made their way down, a violent storm blew in from the northeast. Heavy rains and winds pelted the city. Those still in the tower hurried down the steps to wait out the storm on the ground under the first platform. Many held their breath, hoping that the tower would be as strong as the winds that were buffeting it. To their delight and relief, the tower proved every bit as resilient as Eiffel had advertised. The only thing battered about by the storm was the French flag.

A MOST UNIQUE STRUCTURE

On May 6, 1889, the Paris Universal Exposition officially opened to the public. A large crowd gathered to watch the arrival of French president Sadi Carnot and his entourage at the elaborate iron-and-glass Central Dome, designated as the official entrance to the exposition. At 2 P.M., a brief ceremony was conducted in which the president and the prime minister praised the exposition and welcomed the visitors, which included members of the diplomatic corps who represented a number of the participating countries. In a small ironic twist, Eiffel found himself seated next to one of the tower's most vocal opponents, the architect Charles Garnier. At the ceremony's conclusion, the small group, which included the president, the prime minister, and members of the Exposition Committee, left on a two-mile walk to tour the exposition's major exhibits and attractions.

Not long afterward, some five hundred thousand people crowded through the twenty-two entrances to the grand Paris Exposition. Covering 228 acres, the Paris Exposition was one-third larger than the previous event in 1878. And even though many of the exhibits and buildings were not yet finished, people still marveled at the wonderful sights.

Without a doubt, the hub of the exposition was the Champ de Mars. Among the eye-catching attractions was not only the Eiffel Tower, but the great Palais des Machines.

Gustave Eiffel unfurls the French flag atop his newly constructed tower.

Visitors who continued walking to the Esplanade des Invalides could visit the military exhibits sponsored by the French War Department. Buildings representing the architectural styles of France's Asian and African colonies were also located here. The Trocadéro gardens were the appropriate home for the exposition's horticulture exhibits, while the agricultural and food displays could be found along the Quai d'Orsay.

Later that evening, the opening festivities concluded with an enormous fireworks display along the banks of the Seine River. Despite the fireworks illuminating the night sky, many turned their eyes to the massive beacon flashing alternately blue, red, and white lights on the fairgrounds. The Eiffel Tower was staging a spectacular light show of its own. Periodically, cannons boomed from the tower's platforms, while brightly colored flares burst forth and two large white spotlights sent their beams into the darkened streets of Paris. It was an unforgettable sight.

Those who wished to ascend the tower, though, were in for a long wait. Due to some last-minute touch-up work, the tower did not officially open to the public for another nine days, and even then the elevators were still not fully operational. In the

On May 6, 1889, the Paris Universal Exposition opened to the public.

very first of its special editions that were to be published from its offices in the tower, the newspaper *Le Figaro de la Tour Eiffel* stated: "We have put together this number under rather special conditions: in a shack that barely covers our heads amid carpenters, gas workers, blacksmiths and painters, dizzy from the unaccustomed air, dust and noise and tired by the climb up the equivalent of the 36 stories.[34]

Finally, at 11:50 A.M. on May 15, 1889, Eiffel made a short entry in the tower guest book: "Ten minutes to twelve, May 15, 1889. The tower is opened to the public. At last!"[35] The line of visitors that had formed well over an hour before started to move up the stairs located at the west end of the tower.

A Visit to the Tower

Writer Eugene Reboul captured the initial excitement the tower generated, commenting that "when we arrived in Paris, our first idea was to go and see the tower—I don't need to tell you which tower, do I?"[36] Reboul and his companions were not alone. During the next seven days, nearly 30,000 people paid forty cents for a red ticket that allowed them to visit the first platform of the Eiffel Tower. For an additional twenty cents, visitors could buy a white ticket that entitled them to visit the second platform as well. For one dollar, visitors could ride to the top of the tower in one of the elevators.

Without question, the tower was a sensation. But no one was prepared for the ecstatic response, except perhaps Eiffel himself, who had believed all along that his tower would be a truly spectacular sight. The tower was by far the most popular attraction of the Centennial Exposition. People waited hours for a chance to visit it.

In addition to the breathtaking views, the tower offered an array of activities. Visitors who stopped on the first platform might go to the "land of eating and drinking," as the area had been named, where hungry tourists had their choice of dining. One restaurant featured the fine French cuisine of a famous local eating spot, Brébant's, which also happened to boast one of the best views of the exposition. Restaurants featuring foods from Russia and the province of Alsace-Lorraine were also quite popular. Many tourists enjoyed stopping and having a drink in the Anglo-American bar. Furthermore, there was a 250-seat area in which people could sit, eat, and talk. Merchants sold souvenirs, binoculars, and tobacco.

THE CENTENNIAL EXPOSITION

Although the Eiffel Tower was the runaway sensation of the Paris Centennial Exposition, there were plenty of other things to see and do. More than 32 million people visited the exposition during the six months it was open, making it the most successful world's fair ever. Besides the Eiffel Tower, visitors could view more than sixty thousand exhibits assembled by the representatives of forty-nine countries. Two of the most popular exhibits were from the United States.

The first displayed inventor Thomas Edison's new phonograph machine, which played prerecorded music and sounds on special cylinders. Lines formed early each day outside the exhibit's building as crowds eagerly awaited the chance to listen through a headset to some of the first sound recordings ever made.

The second outstanding American attraction was the appearance of Buffalo Bill Cody's Wild West Show, a rousing spectacle of fancy shooting, daredevil riding stunts, and other exciting exploits as performed by real American cowboys and Indians. Costarring Annie Oakley, the famous American sharpshooter known as "Queen of the Rifle," the show performed twice a day during the exposition. Buffalo Bill's troupe always played to sold-out houses, as thousands of Europeans thrilled to the spectacle of the American West coming alive before their very eyes.

Located on the second platform were the newspaper offices of the *Figaro*, a small bakery, and a refreshment stand. An amazing sight awaited those bold enough to take the elevator to the top level, however. A circular hall opened onto the laboratories that Eiffel had specified be included in the tower. The rooms overlooked a terrace where a small train made its way around a circular track, its cars carrying the huge electric spotlights that shone over the city at night. A spiral staircase led to the fourth platform, to which no one was admitted, for it was the private apartment of Eiffel.

Clear days rewarded visitors with a spectacular view of Paris and its surroundings. Looking in any direction, people could see thirty, forty, and even fifty miles into the distance. To the north lay the Compiègne Forest, to the east, the city of Château-Thierry.

The town of Fontainebleau was to the south, and the plains stretching toward the Normandy coast lay to the west.

Originally, Eiffel had planned for the tower to accommodate 10,000 visitors at once. The restaurants alone seated 400 people each. The numbers of visitors to the tower during the exposition overwhelmed its capacity, however. In the six months the exposition ran, estimates suggest that on average 11,000 people a day visited the tower. The single largest turnout was on June 10, 1889, a holiday, when some 23,000 people came. When the final figures were totaled, it was estimated that 1,968,287 people visited the Eiffel Tower, paying 5,919,884 francs, ($1,142,834) in admission fees, allowing Eiffel to pay off completely the money owed for the tower's construction. So many people came to see

Restaurants on the Eiffel Tower seated four hundred people each.

his creation that at one point Eiffel joked, "I ought to be jealous of the tower, it is much more famous than I am."[37]

People fell in love with the great iron tower and wanted to take away something with which to commemorate their visit. They had themselves photographed in front of it. Some bought replicas of it, while others took home larger likenesses from which to make lamps. Young women, meanwhile, purchased tower charms to attach to bracelets. China plates, goblets, music boxes, and large sea shells all imprinted with images of the tower were for sale. Many visitors also got a special edition of the *Figaro* with their names and the date they had come printed in the corner. Hundreds of thousands from around the world signed the guest book.

LIFE AFTER THE TOWER

As it turned out, the Eiffel Tower was the last major structure that Eiffel built. During its construction, Eiffel became involved in another project that might have made him even more famous than his tower: the Panama Canal. But that experience would never come to pass.

By December 1887 Eiffel and his company were building the patented locks that were to be used in the canal. Less than a year later though, the Panama Canal Company, which had hired Eiffel to design and build the locks, went bankrupt. Faced with increasing financial and technical difficulties, the project was halted. Eiffel stood to lose almost $25 million as a result.

For the next five years, a public investigation into the finances and business practices of the Panama Canal Company as well as Eiffel's company occupied the French Parliament. Eiffel was accused of misusing funds, and during the next several years he spent a great deal of time and money proving his innocence. He was, in the end, cleared of any wrongdoing. But the Panama Canal scandal, and perhaps the strain of building the Eiffel Tower, took its toll. In 1893 Eiffel resigned as chairman of the board of his company and ended his active participation in business.

A WORKING RETIREMENT

Although semiretired, Eiffel spent the next three decades living and working in the tower that bore his name. If anything, this period was in many ways the most creative and fulfilling of his life. Eiffel now had the time to spend on pursuing his many other interests such as meteorology, aerodynamics and aviation, and telecommunications.

After construction of the tower was done, Eiffel had installed a number of thermometers, barometers, and anemometers on the third platform of the tower. Working closely with the French Central Weather Bureau, he systematically monitored patterns and changes in the weather. Instead of having to estimate temperature, wind direction and velocity, and cloud cover, the instruments Eiffel used provided accurate information for scientists to analyze. Eiffel helped with this work by carefully recording his observations in a weather atlas and by establishing his own twenty-five-station weather network. His activities helped to lay the groundwork for the development of modern meteorology in France.

Eiffel (left) conducted meteorological experiments at the top of the tower.

In addition to the weather studies, Eiffel, with the help of his son-in-law, also conducted tests on the effects of high altitudes on the human body. Based on their studies, the two concluded that walking the tower's steps was excellent therapy for those suffering from anemia (lack of energy) and dyspepsia (indigestion). By climbing higher toward the top of the tower, they said one would experience "a feeling of well-being . . . and the irresistible desire to go still higher—in sum, a general excitement which recalls that provoked by visits to mountain resorts."[38] While today these conclusions do not stand up to close scrutiny, in Eiffel's time they were given serious consideration.

In 1903 Eiffel became interested in aviation. Setting up a small laboratory on the second platform of the tower, he made detailed studies of air resistance and experimented with a wind tunnel to learn more about aerodynamic balance, propeller efficiency, and airflow. Eiffel's investigations led him to devise an equation for propeller design that proved invaluable to engineers looking for ways to improve the new flying machines. But as the Champ de Mars area became more popular with city residents and visitors alike, city officials began hearing an increasing number of complaints about the noisy experiments being conducted at the tower. As a result, Eiffel was found to be in violation of the city's zoning law and told to stop using his wind tunnel. While restricted from carrying out his experiments at the tower, Eiffel simply created another lab facility at nearby Auteuil, where he constructed an even bigger wind tunnel. Never one to hoard his secrets, Eiffel would publish his findings. Because of his willingness to share his ideas and data, several European countries, the United States, and Japan utilized Eiffel's ideas in developing their own experiments in aerodynamics.

Eiffel also experimented with early forms of telecommunications. In 1904 he mounted an antenna on the tower that enabled him to send and receive messages within a radius of 250 miles. As a result of this early success, in 1908 Eiffel founded his own radio network, where he communicated with cities in Europe, North Africa, and North America. In time, these early forays in telecommunications led to the establishment of a permanent transmission facility on the Eiffel Tower that is still in use today.

By 1920 Gustave Eiffel was eighty-eight years old and finally beginning to slow down. Besides his numerous building feats and scientific research, he had written thirty-one books, in-

SOME FAMOUS VISITORS

The Eiffel Tower was not only of interest to ordinary tourists. Many notable and famous persons also came to see it. Certainly one of the grandest visitors was the Prince of Wales, later King Edward VII of England, who visited with his family on June 10, 1889. On July 22, the king of Greece paid his respects to Gustave Eiffel. The shah of Persia came twice; the first time to watch his attendants climb to the first platform, the second time to walk the stairs to the first platform by himself; his only comments were that the elevators were much too noisy. The grand duke of Russia shared a glass of champagne in Eiffel's tower apartment with other members of European nobility. Thomas Edison also stopped by and presented one of his phonographs to Eiffel along with a recording of the French national anthem "The Marseillaise." Another noted guest was Frédéric-Auguste Bartholdi, who knew Eiffel well. Bartholdi, designer of the Statue of Liberty, had depended on Eiffel for the statue's iron skeleton, which prevented Lady Liberty from toppling over.

Frédéric-Auguste Bartholdi, designer of the Statue of Liberty, was a noted guest at the Eiffel Tower.

cluding his autobiography. He had also received a number of honorary medals and decorations during the course of his long life, each one acknowledging one of his many achievements. But as Eiffel himself admitted, the Eiffel Tower was his greatest accomplishment. In an interview, Eiffel's grandson, René Le-Grain Eiffel, described his grandfather's feeling for the tower as a "symbol of force and difficulties overcome . . . [an] incomparable monument, the tallest ever to come from the hand of man."[39]

On December 27, 1923, at the age of ninety-one, Gustave Eiffel died peacefully at home. How fortunate for the millions who traveled across his bridges, who waited for trains in one of his terminals, or who visited his tower that this man from Dijon became an engineer rather than a chemist devoted to the fermentation of vinegar.

EPILOGUE

Even after the Centennial Exposition closed, the Eiffel Tower continued to draw large crowds. The tower became not only one of the most popular landmarks in Paris but also one of the most famous and recognized sights in the entire world. In time, the Eiffel Tower came less to symbolize the engineering genius of one man and more to represent an entire nation.

A VIEW TO HISTORY

The Eiffel Tower has been a silent witness to some of the greatest and most terrible events in the history of the twentieth century. The tower was closed between 1915 and 1918 as France and its allies battled Germany in World War I. Eiffel's experiments with telecommunications, however, played an important role during the conflict. In August 1914, the French used the radio equipment located on the tower to intercept a message about the movement of German troops as they advanced toward Paris. This information helped French generals plan their counterattack against the Germans.

During World War II, the tower again served as a communications center for the French army until Paris fell to the Germans in June 1940. Before the Germans could seize control of the tower and its radio transmitters, though, the French destroyed them and, for good measure, disabled the elevator system as well. In 1942, rumors that the Germans planned to dismantle the tower for its metal circulated for months among the residents of Paris. It was said that the Germans in the end decided against the plan for fear that Parisians would rebel in protest.

Even during this time, the tower still proved a popular attraction. German soldiers came in droves to see it, averaging fifteen thousand a day during the German occupation of Paris. Even Adolf Hitler visited the majestic tower. When he learned that the French had destroyed the elevators and he would have to walk the tower steps, Hitler refused and settled instead for having his photograph taken with the tower in the background.

When Allied troops liberated Paris in 1944, American soldiers reinstalled a radio communications center on the tower that helped coordinate Allied military operations outside the city. Allied commanders considered the tower so important to the war effort that the chief signal officer of the U.S. War Department personally wrote Gustave Eiffel's grandson after the war to thank him for allowing the army to use it.

A WORLD ATTRACTION

Despite the interruptions of war, the Eiffel Tower has attracted a steady stream of visitors since it opened more than 100 years ago. It continues to be the most-visited monument in Paris and, indeed, throughout France. Visitors to the tower often surpass the number of tourists who go to such famous landmarks as the Statue of Liberty and the Washington Monument in the United States. In fact, the people who come to visit the Eiffel Tower have even received a special nickname from the French press. They are now known not as tourists, but as "towerists," in recognition of their visits to the Eiffel Tower.

Although attendance fell off just after the end of the Centennial Exposition, it soon picked up again, with

During France's German occupation in World War II, Adolf Hitler (foreground, second from right) had his picture taken at the Eiffel Tower's base.

more than 1 million sightseers visiting the tower eleven years later during the Paris Exposition of 1900. Attendance again declined in 1902 when only 121,444 people came. The numbers then increased until World War I, with an average of about 200,000 people a year. Two years after the end of World War II, in 1947, the tower had more than 1 million visitors for the first time since 1900. With few exceptions, the annual numbers have continued to grow in recent decades. By the end of 1999, for example, estimates suggest that approximately 185,804,990 persons had visited the Eiffel Tower in the 110 years of its existence.

THE TOWER DAY-TO-DAY

Today, the Eiffel Tower is owned and operated by sixteen hundred shareholders of the Société de la Tour Eiffel. Through an arrangement with the city of Paris, the group leases the tower for specified periods of time. When the old lease expires, the shareholders negotiate a new one with the city, an arrangement that

FEATS OF FOLLY AND STUNNING SPECTACLES

The Eiffel Tower has been at the center of some amazing feats of daring as well as stupidity. In 1891 a local baker climbed to the first platform on a pair of stilts. In 1906 a foot race sponsored by a Paris sports newspaper attracted 120 entrants. One of the more ambitious contestants raced to the second platform of the tower carrying one hundred pounds of cement on his shoulders.

In 1923 a bicyclist circled the first floor platform and then rode down the 363 steps from the first level to the ground to the cheers of onlookers. In 1958 a man on a unicycle accomplished the same feat. And many people still talk about the man who, in 1959, hopped up the first level tower stairs on one leg.

During World War II, a U.S. army pilot flew his plane between the tower's pillars, one of many who attempted this feat. He was among the few who succeeded; others have not been so fortunate. Then there have been those who have climbed the Eiffel Tower as if it were a large metal mountain, scaling its metal bracings. In many cases, all these daredevils received for their efforts was a police escort down from the tower and a request never to attempt the climb again. To commemorate the seventy-fifth anniversary of the tower in 1964, however, French cameras televised the ascent of the tower by four experienced mountain climbers.

has worked well since 1889. In return for the lease, the city of Paris receives 18 percent of the gross revenues paid to the company. All of the businesses located on the tower—the restaurants, bar, bistro, and souvenir shops—pay rent to the company. These monies, combined with admission fees, have enabled the tower corporation to enjoy steady profits.

To maintain the tower on a daily basis requires the services of roughly 120 people, including 2 full-time engineer supervisors and 37 technicians. The remaining workers operate the elevators, sell and take tickets, and make sure that everything runs smoothly on each platform.

Every seven years, the tower receives a new coat of paint. To paint the tower, or "give her a new dress" as the Parisians refer to the process, is the largest maintenance job done to the tower. The project requires some thirty professional painters. First they scrub off the grime that has accumulated since the last painting, and then sand and touch up any rust spots that have appeared. Next the painters apply with brushes fifty-five tons of a special silicon and lead paint. Although the painters take great care not to drip paint, occasionally passersby on the streets below are the unhappy recipients of an unwanted drop or two.

Sometimes, sections of the tower need to be repaired or replaced. When that happens, workers using closed-circuit televisions, pinpoint the areas that need work. Going carefully over every bolt and rivet helps the engineers make precise evaluations of the strength and stability of the tower.

Keeping the tower in good shape is expensive. On average, five hundred thousand dollars is spent annually on maintenance and upkeep.

Every seven years, the Eiffel Tower gets a new coat of paint.

In 1933 the world's biggest clock, measuring fifty feet in diameter, was installed in the tower.

THE WORLD'S BRIGHTEST AND THE WORLD'S LARGEST . . .

Certainly one of the most exciting sights in Paris is the tower lit up at night. On July 4, 1925, the tower was illuminated for the first time when a local automobile dealer received permission to use the tower to advertise his cars. For the next few years, thousands of colored electric lights were added to give the illusion of waterfalls and colored fountains spraying from the tower. The electric light displays were so grand that they even provided aviator Charles Lindbergh with a landmark on his famous nonstop flight from New York to Paris in 1927.

For years, the electric light displays were some of the most spectacular in the world. Even so, in 1985 the Parisians managed to improve the tower's light display. That year, a different type of lighting system was installed. Three hundred and fifty-two special projectors that gave off a yellow orange light were placed in the interior of the tower. The result was a lighting display that makes the tower stand out even more brilliantly than it did before.

The Eiffel Tower has also had some of the world's largest objects attached to it during its existence. For instance, in 1933 the world's biggest clock was installed in the tower. Fifty feet in diameter, the hands of the clock were actually colored lights showing the hour and minute. In 1934 a thermometer made of electric lights was also attached to the tower. Stretching from the second platform to the top, the thermometer had a series of white lights situated every eight feet surrounding a string of red lights, acting as the mercury level and indicating the temperature of the air around the tower.

The Eiffel Tower has also served as a perfect backdrop for numerous fireworks displays, most recently for the millennium celebration on December 31, 1999. From eighty platforms on the tower,

New Year's Eve celebrants were treated to one hundred different types of fireworks. Many observers agreed that of all the millennium events, the Eiffel Tower celebration was by far the best.

The tower also has been the site for everything from classical music concerts and beauty contests to angry protests by workers, students, and farmers. It has provided inspiration for artists, novelists, poets, playwrights, and filmmakers the world over. The tower even gets mail from people wanting to know its history or wishing it a happy birthday. Images of the tower continue to be reproduced on everything from posters to plates. Even a casino in Las Vegas, Nevada, has built a fifty-story replica of the tower as part of its hotel. Models of the tower are everywhere, from the official souvenirs one can buy to models constructed of eleven thousand toothpicks to another built of more than 2 million matchsticks.

MORE THAN JUST A TOWER

Since the tower's construction, bigger and taller buildings have been erected. It is no longer the world's tallest tower, yet the Eiffel Tower continues to fascinate people around the world. For many, the tower symbolizes one of man's greatest engineering feats. To others, the Eiffel Tower stands as the first truly modern structure in the world. Many of the buildings and structures of today owe a great debt to Eiffel's techniques and use of new building materials.

For the French, the Eiffel Tower represents much more than technological achievements. What began as an object of humor and ridicule has grown over the past century to become the symbol of France. The Eiffel Tower showed the world in 1889 a new and modern France, a country ready to compete with the other industrialized nations of Europe. Yet it took the French a long time to decide officially that the Eiffel Tower was an important part of their heritage. Finally, in 1964 the French government

Images of the tower are reproduced in many ways, from tiny replicas to paintings to plates.

A truly modern structure, the Eiffel Tower stands as a national treasure and symbol of French "know-how."

recognized what so many already knew; the Eiffel Tower was a cherished national monument. In declaring the tower a national treasure, the French government protected it from ever being changed without special permission. As one French writer explained: "Notre Dame represents the Faith, the Institute [National] and University are the life of the mind, the Panthéon is service rendered to the nation, the Élysee Palace symbolizes the State, the Louvre art and history, the Arch of Triumph and the Invalides mean glory. . . .The Eiffel Tower, so often criticized . . . symbolize[s] the vitality of our know-how."[40]

NOTES

Introduction

1. Miriam R. Levin, *When the Eiffel Tower Was New*. South Hadley, MA: Mount Holyoke College Art Museum, 1989, p. 23.

Chapter 1: The Idea of a Tower

2. Quoted in J. H. Hexter et al., *Europe Since 1500*. Harper and Row, 1971, p. 848.

3. Quoted in Hexter et al., *Europe Since 1500*, p. 848.

4. Quoted in Joseph Harriss, *The Tallest Tower*. Boston: Houghton Mifflin, 1975, p. 6.

5. Quoted in Harriss, *The Tallest Tower*, 1975, p. 8.

6. Quoted in Harriss, *The Tallest Tower*, 1975, p. 14.

7. Quoted in Harriss, *The Tallest Tower*, 1975, p. 11.

8. Quoted in Vilma Barr, "Alexandre Gustave Eiffel: A Towering Engineering Genius," *Mechanical Engineering-CIME*, February 1992.

9. Quoted in Henri Loyette, *Gustave Eiffel*. New York: Rizzoli International Publications, 1985, p. 116.

Chapter 2: An Engineering Genius

10. Quoted in Loyette, *Gustave Eiffel*, p. 23.

11. Quoted in Loyette, *Gustave Eiffel*, p. 25.

12. Quoted in Loyette, *Gustave Eiffel*, p. 29.

13. Quoted in Loyette, *Gustave Eiffel*, p. 29.

14. Quoted in Loyette, *Gustave Eiffel*, p. 29.

15. Quoted in Loyette, *Gustave Eiffel*, p. 32.

16. Quoted in Harriss, *The Tallest Tower*, p. 37.

17. Quoted in Harriss, *The Tallest Tower*, p. 104.

18. Quoted in Harriss, *The Tallest Tower*, p. 45.

Chapter 3: A Work in Progress

19. Quoted in Loyette, *Gustave Eiffel*, p. 119.

20. Quoted in Loyette, *Gustave Eiffel*, p. 119.

21. Quoted in Harriss, *The Tallest Tower*, p. 19.

22. Quoted in Loyette, *Gustave Eiffel*, p. 172.

23. Quoted in Harriss, *The Tallest Tower*, p. 20.

24. Quoted in Harriss, *The Tallest Tower*, p. 20.

25. Quoted in Harriss, *The Tallest Tower*, p. 23.

26. Quoted in Loyette, *Gustave Eiffel*, p. 176.

27. Quoted in Loyette, *Gustave Eiffel*, p. 176.

28. Quoted in Harriss, *The Tallest Tower*, p. 25.

Chapter 4: A Dizzily Ridiculous Tower

29. Quoted in Loyette, *Gustave Eiffel*, p. 148.

30. Quoted in Harriss, *The Tallest Tower*, p. 67.

31. Quoted in Loyette, *Gustave Eiffel*, p. 139.

32. Quoted in Harriss, *The Tallest Tower*, p. 76.

33. Quoted in Harriss, *The Tallest Tower*, p. 81.

Chapter 5: "More Famous Than I Am"

34. Quoted in Harriss, *The Tallest Tower*, p. 116.

35. Quoted in Harriss, *The Tallest Tower*, p. 116.

36. Quoted in Loyette, *Gustave Eiffel*, p. 150.

37. Quoted in Barr, "Alexandre Gustave Eiffel."

38. Quoted in Harriss, *The Tallest Tower*, p. 163.

39. Quoted in Harriss, *The Tallest Tower*, p. 175.

Epilogue

40. Quoted in Harriss, *The Tallest Tower*, p. 215.

GLOSSARY

abutment: A support for the edge of a bridge or other structure.

arch girder: A beam formed with a curve.

caisson: A watertight chamber in which underwater construction can be done.

cast iron: A hard, brittle iron made with carbon used for structural and decorative construction.

deck: The floor of a bridge.

gallery: A long narrow hallway, a building or hall used for displays.

girder: A structural component or part that, used horizontally, acts as one of the major supports for a building or bridges.

gorge: A narrow opening between hills, or a rocky ravine.

hydraulic: Through the use of pressure, the moving of liquids such as water or oil through pipes.

hydraulic presses: Machinery using hydraulic power for construction.

lattice girders: Metal beams with a lattice or screenlike pattern.

lattice trusses: Two parallel metal beams linked by small metal bars arranged in a zigzag pattern.

masonry: Constructed of stone or brick.

minaret: A turret or tower.

nave: A central space, often of a church, that is adjoined by side aisles.

parabola: A curve formed by the set of equidistant points from a given line and a given point on the line.

pier: A square or rectangular post or support often made of masonry or wood that carries the weight of the entire structure.

pile: A heavy vertical beam, usually placed in soft ground, that supports the foundations of a superstructure

pile driving: The process, by special machinery, of driving piles into the ground.

prefabricated: Built or manufactured parts made in advance.

pylon: A tall structure used for support.

rivet: A short pin of iron, steel, or copper with a head on one end, used to join two metal plates.

span: The distance, or structural part, between two supports.

transept: A space that crosses at a right angle to a nave, also known as a wing.

truss: A type of bracing or framework often found in bridges.

vaulted: An arched ceiling or roof structure.

ziggurat: A Mesopotamian temple tower.

For Further Reading

Books

Winnie Denker and Françoise Sagan, *The Eiffel Tower*. New York: Vendome Press, 1989. This book, published on the centennial of the tower's opening, looks at the tower during its first one hundred years.

Henri Loyette, *Gustave Eiffel*. New York: Rizzoli International Publications, 1985. A well-done biography of Gustave Eiffel that covers his entire career. Has a number of excellent photographs detailing the tower's construction.

Periodicals

Jean-Pierre Navailles, "Eiffel's Tower," *History Today*, December 1989. An excellent overview of the tower's construction and its controversy.

WORKS CONSULTED

Books

Roland Barthes, *The Eiffel Tower*. New York: Hill and Wang, 1979. A collection of essays, one of which discusses the impact and influence of the Eiffel Tower.

David P. Billington, *The Tower and the Bridge*. New York: Basic Books, 1983. In this book, the author explores some of the greatest engineering structures ever built, including the Eiffel Tower.

Joseph Harriss, *The Tallest Tower*. Boston: Houghton Mifflin, 1975. An excellent biography of Gustave Eiffel that looks at his entire career, with a special focus on the Eiffel Tower and the Centennial Exposition.

Erwin Heinle and Fritz Leonhardt, *Towers: A Historical Survey*. New York: Rizzoli International Publications, 1989. What is the fascination with towers? This books explores why people build tall buildings. An interesting architectural history of towers from their earliest beginnings to contemporary buildings.

J. H. Hexter et al., *Europe Since 1500*. New York: Harper & Row, 1971. A European history survey that provides background on France in the late nineteenth century and the Belle Epoque.

Miriam R. Levin, *When the Eiffel Tower Was New*. South Hadley, MA: Mount Holyoke College Art Museum, 1989. This book was published in conjunction with an art exhibit that explored the art and history of the Centennial Exposition.

B. Marrey, *Gustave Eiffel and His Times*. Paris: Musée de la Poste, 1983. This catalog was done in conjunction with an exhibit on Gustave Eiffel and his work.

Elizabeth Mock, *The Architecture of Bridges*. New York: Museum of Modern Art, 1949. A helpful architectural history of bridge construction.

Lewis Mumford, *The Brown Decades*. New York: Harcourt, Brace, 1931. A look at nineteenth- and early-twentieth-century architectural history.

Periodicals

Vilma Barr, "Alexandre Gustave Eiffel: A Towering Engineering Genius," *Mechanical Engineering-CIME*, February 1992. A short overview of the life and works of Gustave Eiffel.

Joseph Barry, "Eiffel, Versatile Engineer-Builder of Towering Talents," *Smithsonian*, April 1972. A look at the life and work of Gustave Eiffel.

J. Bryan, "The Eiffel Tower," *Holiday*, May 1955. A short history of the tower and its appeal as a tourist attraction.

Peter Ames Carlin and Cathy Nolan, "Eiffel Power," *People*, January 24, 2000. Preparations for the millennium celebration for the Eiffel Tower are the subject of this article.

"Cashing In on Its 75 Years, " *Business Week*, May 16, 1964. A short article on how the Eiffel Tower is doing as a major tourist attraction on the seventy-fifth anniversary of its construction.

Don Cook, "Landmark on the Seine," *Saturday Evening Post*, August 11, 1962. An article on the popularity and history of the tower.

"French Farmers Gather at the Eiffel Tower to Protest Globalization," *AP Worldstream*, November 30, 1999. A short article about a protest by French farmers in front of the Eiffel Tower.

"Gold Mine in the Sky," *Newsweek*, June 18 1962. The appeal of the Eiffel Tower and why it continues to attract tourists.

Dennis Karwatka, "Gustave Eiffel and His Tower," *Tech Directions*, October 1999. This article looks at the life and accomplishments of Gustave Eiffel, particularly the Eiffel Tower. Special attention is paid to Eiffel's scientific research after he retired.

"Paris Recalls Building of 'Loathsome' Eiffel Tower, " *Life*, July 3, 1950. A look back at some of the reasons why people did not want the tower built.

Jason Straziuso, "Millennium Plays on at Eiffel Tower," *Los Angeles Times*, May 7, 2000. Description of the first symphony concert ever held at the Eiffel Tower.

Web Sites

Eiffel Tower: Facts, News, and Information. www.endex.com/gf/ buildings/eiffel/eiffel.html. This web page is full of information about the tower.

Official Site of The Eiffel Tower. www.tour-eiffel.fr/tour_uk/. Find out how many people have visited the tower since it first opened, its history, and other interesting bits of information; the site also provides information on the tower's hours of operation, ticket prices, and other special events.

INDEX

restaurants, 69, 71
Revolution of 1789, 57
rivets, 52–53
rollers, 34
Roux, Combaluzier, and Lepape, 63
Royal Society of Arts, 12
Russia, grand duke of, 75

St. Petersburg, 29
Sainte Barbé college, 27
School of Arts and Letters. *See* Conservatoire des Arts et Métiers
Seine River, 22, 28, 50–51, 56, 68
Seine valley, 42
Seyrig, Théophile, 32
Sioule Bridge, 33
skeletal framing, 11
Société de la Tour Eiffel, 77
soil samples, 50
Souppes-sur-Loing quarry, 52
spires, 11
spotlights, 63
Statue of Liberty, 38–39, 75, 77
steel, 40
stunts, 78
Suez Canal, 32

Tallest Tower, The (Harriss), 45, 60
Tan An Bridge, 37
Tay Bridge accident, 37
Technical College. *See* École Polytechnique, 27–29
telecommunications, 73
Thailand, 17
thermometers, 73, 80
Thiers, Adolphe, 15–17

train stations, 37–38
Treaty of Frankfurt, 15
Trevithick, Richard, 20
Trocadéro gardens, 22, 43–44, 68
Truyere River, 34–35

United States
    France gives Statue of Liberty to, 38–39
    uses Gustave's ideas for aerodynamics, 74
Universal Exposition of the Products of Industry. *See* Centennial Exposition (France)
U.S. War Department, 76

vertigo (loss of balance), 48
Viana Bridge, 36–37
Victoria, Queen, 12
Vienna, 29
Vietnam, 17
Vogüé, Vicomte de, 55

wages for workers, 58
Washington Monument, 21, 42, 77
water sprinklers, 22
Wild West Show, 70
wind tunnels, 74
windmills, 12
work-site party, 66–67
world's fairs. *See* industrial fairs
World War I and II, 76
wrought iron, 33–35, 40

ziggurats (heavenly mountains), 10–11
Zola, Émile, 21

# Picture Credits

Cover photo: (main picture), PhotoDisc, (gear), Archive Photos, (small picture), Archive France/Tallandier
Archive Photos/Hulton Getty, 16, 17, 23, 59, 62, 71, 73, 75, 77
Art Resource, 10
Brown Brothers, 8, 45
Corbis, 54
Corbis/ Bettmann, 64
Corbis/Leonard de Silva, 47
Corbis/Seth Joel, 31
Corbis/David Langfield/Eye Ubiquitous, 35
Corbis/Hans Georg Roth, 27
Corbis/Underwood and Underwood, 41
Corbis/Michael S. Yamashita, 44
FPG Intl., 9, 39, 51, 79, 80
FPG Intl./Ron Chapple, 81
FPG Intl./Dennie Cody, 53
FPG Intl./Michael Goldman, 65
FPG Intl./Photoworld, 68
FPG Intl./Chris Salvo, 56
PhotoDisc, 12, 28, 82
Stock Montage, Inc., 13, 25, 32, 67

ABOUT THE AUTHOR

Meg Greene is a writer and historian with a particular interest in late-nineteenth- and early-twentieth-century architecture. She has a B.S. in history from Lindenwood College, an M.A. in history from the University of Nebraska–Omaha, and an M.S. in historic preservation from the University of Vermont. She is the author of seven books, one of which *Slave Young, Slave Long*, was recognized as a 1999 Honor Book from the Society of School Librarians International for Grades 7–12. She is a regular contributor to *Cobblestone* magazine, and a Contributing Editor to "History For Children," for Suite 101.com. Ms. Greene makes her home in Virginia.